Practical Computer Vision

Extract insightful information from images using TensorFlow, Keras, and OpenCV

Abhinav Dadhich

BIRMINGHAM - MUMBAI

Practical Computer Vision

Commissioning Editor: Amey Varangaonkar
Acquisition Editor: Aman Singh
Content Development Editor: Snehal Kolte
Technical Editor: Sayli Nikalje
Copy Editor: Safis Editing
Project Coordinator: Manthan Patel
Proofreader: Safis Editing
Indexer: Rekha Nair
Graphics: Tania Dutta
Production Coordinator: Nilesh Mohite

First published: February 2018

Production reference: 1020218

Published by Packt Publishing Ltd.
Livery Place
35 Livery Street
Birmingham
B3 2PB, UK.

ISBN 978-1-78829-768-4

www.packtpub.com

This book is dedicated to my grandfather and in memory of my grandmother.

With love,
-Abhinav

`mapt.io`

Mapt is an online digital library that gives you full access to over 5,000 books and videos, as well as industry leading tools to help you plan your personal development and advance your career. For more information, please visit our website.

Why subscribe?

- Spend less time learning and more time coding with practical eBooks and Videos from over 4,000 industry professionals

- Improve your learning with Skill Plans built especially for you

- Get a free eBook or video every month

- Mapt is fully searchable

- Copy and paste, print, and bookmark content

PacktPub.com

Did you know that Packt offers eBook versions of every book published, with PDF and ePub files available? You can upgrade to the eBook version at `www.PacktPub.com` and as a print book customer, you are entitled to a discount on the eBook copy. Get in touch with us at `service@packtpub.com` for more details.

At `www.PacktPub.com`, you can also read a collection of free technical articles, sign up for a range of free newsletters, and receive exclusive discounts and offers on Packt books and eBooks.

Contributors

About the author

Abhinav Dadhich is a Researcher and Application Developer on deep learning at Abeja Inc. Tokyo. His day is often filled with designing deep learning models for computer vision applications like image classification, object detection, segmentation etc. His passion lies in understanding and replicating human vision system. Previously, he has worked on 3D mapping and robot navigation. He has graduated with B.Tech. in EE from IIT Jodhpur, India and has done his M.Eng. in Information Science from NAIST, Japan. He puts up notes and codes for several topics on GitHub profile.

I would like to thank my family, mom, dad, and sister, for always encouraging me to work harder and supporting me throughout the book writing sessions. Also, I want to thank my Professors for teaching me the hard stuff in computer vision and improving my understanding. I would like to finally thank my reviewers for providing valuable suggestions towards the improvement of this book.

About the reviewer

Nishanth Koganti received a BTech in electrical engineering from the Indian Institute of Technology, Jodhpur, India, in 2012, He completed his ME and PhD in information science from the Nara Institute of Science and Technology, Japan, in 2014 and 2017 respectively. He is currently a postdoctoral researcher at the University of Tokyo, Japan. His research interests are assistive robotics, motor skills learning, and machine learning. His graduate research was on the development of a clothing assistance robot that helps elderly people wear clothes.

Packt is searching for authors like you

If you're interested in becoming an author for Packt, please visit `authors.packtpub.com` and apply today. We have worked with thousands of developers and tech professionals, just like you, to help them share their insight with the global tech community. You can make a general application, apply for a specific hot topic that we are recruiting an author for, or submit your own idea.

Table of Contents

Preface

Computer vision is one of the most widely studied sub-fields of computer science. It has several important applications, such as face detection, image searching, and artistic image conversion. With the popularity of deep learning methods, many recent applications of computer vision are in self-driving cars, robotics, medicine, Virtual reality, and Augmented reality. In this book, a practical approach of learning computer vision is shown. Using code blocks as well as a theoretical understanding of algorithms will help in building stronger computer vision fundamentals. This book teaches you how to create applications using standard tools such as OpenCV, Keras, and TensorFlow. The various concepts and implementations explained in this book can be used across several domains, such as robotics, image editing apps, and self-driving cars. In this book, each chapter is explained with accompanying code and results to enforce the learning together.

Who this book is for

This book is for undergraduate students and professionals who want to get started with computer vision and gain with a practical knowledge of implementing several of these algorithms. This book assumes that readers have a basic knowledge of Python and computer programs, they can write and run Python scripts (including scientific Python), and they can understand linear algebra and basic mathematics for programming.

This book will help readers in designing newer computer vision applications using image filtering, object detection, segmentation, tracking, and SLAM. Readers will understand the standard computer vision techniques used in the industry, as well as how to write their own code. Do the same as what with widely used libraries. They can use this to create their own applications across various domains, including image filtering, manipulating images, object detection, and advanced applications using deep learning. Readers will find a smooth transition from getting to know computer vision to using advanced techniques.

What this book covers

`Chapter 1`, *A Fast Introduction to Computer Vision*, gives a brief overview of what constitutes computer vision, its applications in different fields and subdivision of different type problems. The chapter also covers basic image input reading with code in OpenCV. There is also an overview of different color spaces and their visualizations.

Chapter 2, *Libraries, Development Platforms, and Datasets*, provides detailed instructions on how to set up a development environment and install libraries inside it. The various datasets introduced in this chapter include both that will be used in this book as well as currently popular datasets for each sub-domain of computer vision. The chapter includes links for downloading and loading wrappers to be used libraries such as Keras.

Chapter 3, *Image Filtering and Transformations in OpenCV*, explains different filtering techniques, including linear and nonlinear filters, their implementation in OpenCV. This chapter also includes techniques for transforming an image, such as linear translation, rotation around a given axis, and complete affine transformation. The techniques introduced in the chapter help in creating applications across several domains and enhancing image quality.

Chapter 4, *What is a Feature?* introduces the features and their importance in various applications in computer vision. The chapter consists of Harris Corner Detectors with basic features, the fast feature detector, and ORB features for both robust and fast features. There are also demonstrations in OpenCV of applications that use these. The applications include matching a template to the original image and matching two images of the same object. There is also a discussion of the black box feature and its necessity.

Chapter 5, *Convolutional Neural Networks*, begins with an introduction to simple neural networks and their components. The chapter also introduces convolutional neural networks in Keras with various components such as activation, pooling, and fully-connected. Results with parameter changes for each component are explained; these can be easily reproduced by the reader. This understanding is further strengthened by implementing a simple CNN model using an image dataset. Along with popular CNN architectures, VGG, Inception, and ResNet, there is an introduction to transfer learning. This leads to a look at state-of-the-art deep learning models for image classification.

Chapter 6, *Feature-Based Object Detection*, develops an understanding of the image recognition problem. Detection algorithms, such as face detectors, are explained with OpenCV. You will also see some recent and popular deep learning-based object detection algorithms such as FasterRCNN, SSD, and others. The effectiveness of each of these is explained with TensorFlow object detection API on custom images.

Chapter 7, *Segmentation and Tracking*, consists of two parts. The first introduces the image instance recognition problem, with an implementation of the deep learning model for segmentation. The second part begins with an introduction to the MOSSE tracker from OpenCV, which is both efficient and fast. An introduction to the deep learning-based tracking of multiple objects is described in tracking.

Chapter 8, *3D Computer Vision*, describes analyzing images from a geometrical point of view. Readers will first understand the challenges in computing depth from a single image, and later learn how to solve them using multiple images. The chapter also describes the way to track a camera pose for moving cameras using visual odometry. Lastly, the SLAM problem is introduced, with solutions presented using the visual SLAM technique, which uses only camera images as input.

Appendix A, *Mathematics for Computer Vision*, introduces basic concepts required in understanding computer vision algorithms. Matrix and vector operations introduced here are further augmented with Python implementations. The appendix also contains an introduction to probability theory with explanations to various distributions.

Appendix B, *Machine Learning for Computer Vision*, gives an overview of machine learning modeling and various key terms involved. The readers will also understand the curse of dimensionality, the various preprocessing and postprocessing involved. There are also explanation on several evaluation tools and methods for machine learning models which are also used quite extensively for vision applications

To get the most out of this book

1. The list of software needed for this book is as follows:
    - Anaconda distribution v5.0.1
    - OpenCV v3.3.0
    - TensorFlow v1.4.0
    - Keras v2.1.2

2. To run all of the code effectively, Ubuntu 16.04 is preferable, with Nvidia GPU and at least 4 GB of RAM. The code will also run without GPU support.

Download the example code files

You can download the example code files for this book from your account at www.packtpub.com. If you purchased this book elsewhere, you can visit www.packtpub.com/support and register to have the files emailed directly to you.

You can download the code files by following these steps:

1. Log in or register at `www.packtpub.com`.
2. Select the **SUPPORT** tab.
3. Click on **Code Downloads & Errata**.
4. Enter the name of the book in the **Search** box and follow the onscreen instructions.

Once the file is downloaded, please make sure that you unzip or extract the folder using the latest version of:

- WinRAR/7-Zip for Windows
- Zipeg/iZip/UnRarX for Mac
- 7-Zip/PeaZip for Linux

The code bundle for the book is also hosted on GitHub at `https://github.com/PacktPublishing/Practical-Computer-Vision`. We also have other code bundles from our rich catalog of books and videos available at `https://github.com/PacktPublishing/`. Check them out!

Download the color images

We also provide a PDF file that has color images of the screenshots/diagrams used in this book. You can download it here: `https://www.packtpub.com/sites/default/files/downloads/PracticalComputerVision_ColorImages.pdf`.

Conventions used

There are a number of text conventions used throughout this book.

`CodeInText`: Indicates code words in text, database table names, folder names, filenames, file extensions, pathnames, dummy URLs, user input, and Twitter handles. Here is an example: "This will install the Python libraries in the `$HOME/anaconda3` folder since we are using Python 3. A Python 2 version is also available and the installation process is similar. To use Anaconda, the newly installed libraries need to be added in `$PATH`, this can be done every time a new shell is launched."

A block of code is set as follows:

```
import numpy as np
import matplotlib.pyplot as plt
import cv2
```

When we wish to draw your attention to a particular part of a code block, the relevant lines or items are set in bold:

```
from sklearn.metrics import f1_score
true_y = .... # ground truth values
pred_y = .... # output of the model

f1_value = f1_score(true_y, pred_y, average='micro')
```

Any command-line input or output is written as follows:

```
sudo apt-get install build-essential
sudo apt-get install cmake git libgtk2.0-dev pkg-config libavcodec-dev
libavformat-dev libswscale-dev
sudo apt-get install libtbb2 libtbb-dev libjpeg-dev libpng-dev libtiff-
dev libjasper-dev libdc1394-22-dev
```

Bold: Indicates a new term, an important word, or words that you see onscreen.

Warnings or important notes appear like this.

Tips and tricks appear like this.

Get in touch

Feedback from our readers is always welcome.

General feedback: Email feedback@packtpub.com and mention the book title in the subject of your message. If you have questions about any aspect of this book, please email us at questions@packtpub.com.

Errata: Although we have taken every care to ensure the accuracy of our content, mistakes do happen. If you have found a mistake in this book, we would be grateful if you would report this to us. Please visit www.packtpub.com/submit-errata, selecting your book, clicking on the Errata Submission Form link, and entering the details.

Piracy: If you come across any illegal copies of our works in any form on the Internet, we would be grateful if you would provide us with the location address or website name. Please contact us at copyright@packtpub.com with a link to the material.

If you are interested in becoming an author: If there is a topic that you have expertise in and you are interested in either writing or contributing to a book, please visit authors.packtpub.com.

Reviews

Please leave a review. Once you have read and used this book, why not leave a review on the site that you purchased it from? Potential readers can then see and use your unbiased opinion to make purchase decisions, we at Packt can understand what you think about our products, and our authors can see your feedback on their book. Thank you!

For more information about Packt, please visit packtpub.com.

1
A Fast Introduction to Computer Vision

Computer vision applications have become quite ubiquitous in our lives. The applications are varied, ranging from apps that play **Virtual Reality (VR)** or **Augmented Reality (AR)** games to applications for scanning documents using smartphone cameras. On our smartphones, we have QR code scanning and face detection, and now we even have facial recognition techniques. Online, we can now search using images and find similar looking images. Photo sharing applications can identify people and make an album based on the friends or family found in the photos. Due to improvements in image stabilization techniques, even with shaky hands, we can create stable videos.

With the recent advancements in deep learning techniques, applications like image classification, object detection, tracking, and so on have become more accurate and this has led to the development of more complex autonomous systems, such as drones, self-driving cars, humanoids, and so on. Using deep learning, images can be transformed into more complex details; for example, images can be converted into Van Gogh style paintings.

Such progress in several domains makes a non-expert wonder, how computer vision is capable of inferring this information from images. The motivation lies in human perception and the way we can perform complex analyzes of the environment around us. We can estimate the closeness of, structure and shape of objects, and estimate the textures of a surface too. Even under different lights, we can identify objects and even recognize something if we have seen it before.

Considering these advancements and motivations, one of the basic questions that arises is what is computer vision? In this chapter, we will begin by answering this question and then provide a broader overview of the various sub-domains and applications within computer vision. Later in the chapter, we will start with basic **image operations**.

What constitutes computer vision?

In order to begin the discussion on computer vision, observe the following image:

Even if we have never done this activity before, we can clearly tell that the image is of people skiing in the snowy mountains on a cloudy day. This information that we perceive is quite complex and can be sub divided into more basic inferences for a computer vision system.

The most basic observation that we can get from an image is of the things or objects in it. In the previous image, the various things that we can see are trees, mountains, snow, sky, people, and so on. Extracting this information is often referred to as image classification, where we would like to label an image with a predefined set of categories. In this case, the labels are the things that we see in the image.

A wider observation that we can get from the previous image is landscape. We can tell that the image consists of **Snow**, **Mountain**, and **Sky**, as shown in the following image:

Although it is difficult to create exact boundaries for where the **Snow**, **Mountain**, and **Sky** are in the image, we can still identify approximate regions of the image for each of them. This is often termed as segmentation of an image, where we break it up into regions according to object occupancy.

Making our observation more concrete, we can further identify the exact boundaries of objects in the image, as shown in the following figure:

In the image, we see that people are doing different activities and as such have different shapes; some are sitting, some are standing, some are skiing. Even with this many variations, we can detect objects and can create bounding boxes around them. Only a few bounding boxes are shown in the image for understanding—we can observe much more than these.

While, in the image, we show rectangular bounding boxes around some objects, we are not categorizing what object is in the box. The next step would be to say the box contains a person. This combined observation of detecting and categorizing the box is often referred to as object detection.

Extending our observation of people and surroundings, we can say that different people in the image have different heights, even though some are nearer and others are farther from the camera. This is due to our intuitive understanding of image formation and the relations of objects. We know that a tree is usually much taller than a person, even if the trees in the image are shorter than the people nearer to the camera. Extracting the information about geometry in the image is another sub-field of computer vision, often referred to as image reconstruction.

Computer vision is everywhere

In the previous section, we developed an initial understanding of computer vision. With this understanding, there are several algorithms that have been developed and are used in industrial applications. Studying these not only improve our understanding of the system but can also seed newer ideas to improve overall systems.

In this section, we will extend our understanding of computer vision by looking at various applications and their problem formulations:

- **Image classification**: In the past few years, categorizing images based on the objects within has gained popularity. This is due to advances in algorithms as well as the availability of large datasets. Deep learning algorithms for image classification have significantly improved the accuracy while being trained on datasets like `ImageNet`. We will study this dataset further in the next chapter. The trained model is often further used to improve other recognition algorithms like object detection, as well as image categorization in online applications. In this book, we will see how to create a simple algorithm to classify images using deep learning models.
- **Object detection**: Not just self-driving cars, but robotics, automated retail stores, traffic detection, smartphone camera apps, image filters and many more applications use object detection. These also benefit from deep learning and vision techniques as well as the availability of large, annotated datasets. We saw an introduction to object detection in the previous section that produces bounding boxes around objects and also categorize what object is inside the box.
- **Object tracking**: Following robots, surveillance cameras and people interaction are few of the several applications of object tracking. This consists of defining the location and keeps track of corresponding objects across a sequence of images.

- **Image geometry**: This is often referred to as computing the depth of objects from the camera. There are several applications in this domain too. Smartphones apps are now capable of computing three-dimensional structures from the video created onboard. Using the three-dimensional reconstructed digital models, further extensions like AR or VR application are developed to interface the image world with the real world.

- **Image segmentation**: This is creating cluster regions in images, such that one cluster has similar properties. The usual approach is to cluster image pixels belonging to the same object. Recent applications have grown in self-driving cars and healthcare analysis using image regions.

- **Image generation**: These have a greater impact in the artistic domain, merging different image styles or generating completely new ones. Now, we can mix and merge Van Gogh's painting style with smartphone camera images to create images that appear as if they were painted in a similar style to Van Gogh's.

The field is quickly evolving, not only through making newer methods of image analysis but also finding newer applications where computer vision can be used. Therefore, applications are not just limited to those explained previously.

Developing vision applications requires significant knowledge of tools and techniques. In Chapter 2, *Libraries, Development Platform, and Datasets*, we will see a list of tools that helps in implementing vision techniques. One of the popular tools for this is OpenCV, which consists of most common algorithms of computer vision. For more recent techniques such as deep learning, Keras and TensorFlow can be used in creating applications.

Though we will see an introductory image operations in the next section, in Chapter 3, *Image Filtering and Transformations in OpenCV*, there are more elaborate image operations of filtering and transformations. These act as initial operations in many applications to remove unwanted information.

In Chapter 4, *What is a Feature?*, we will be introduced to the features of an image. There are several properties in an image such as corners, edges, and so on that can act as key points. These properties are used to find similarities between images. We will implement and understand common features and feature extractors.

The recent advances in vision techniques for image classification or object detection use advanced features that utilize deep-learning-based approaches. In Chapter 5, *Convolutional Neural Networks*, we will begin with understanding various components of a convolutional neural network and how it can be used to classify images.

Object detection, as explained before, is a more complex problem of both localizing the position of an object in an image as well as saying what type of object it is. This, therefore, requires more complex techniques, which we will see in Chapter 6, *Feature-Based Object Detection*, using TensorFlow.

If we would like to know the region of an object in an image, we need to perform image segmentation. In Chapter 7, *Segmentation and Tracking*, we will see some techniques for image segmentation using convolutional neural networks and also techniques for tracking multiple objects in a sequence of images or video.

Finally in Chapter 8, *3D Computer Vision*, there is an introduction to image construction and an application of image geometry, such as visual odometry and visual slam.

Though we will introduce setting up OpenCV in the next chapter in detail, in the next section we will use OpenCV to perform basic image operations of reading and converting images. These operations will show how an image is represented in the digital world and what needs to be changed to improve image quality. More detailed image operations are covered in Chapter 3, *Image Filtering and Transformations in OpenCV*.

Getting started

In this section, we will see basic image operations for reading and writing images. We will also see how images are represented digitally.

Before we proceed further with image IO, let's see what an image is made up of in the digital world. An image is simply a two-dimensional array, with each cell of the array containing intensity values. A simple image is a black and white image with 0's representing white and 1's representing black. This is also referred to as a binary image. A further extension of this is dividing black and white into a broader grayscale with a range of 0 to 255. An image of this type, in the three-dimensional view, is as follows, where x and y are pixel locations and z is the intensity value:

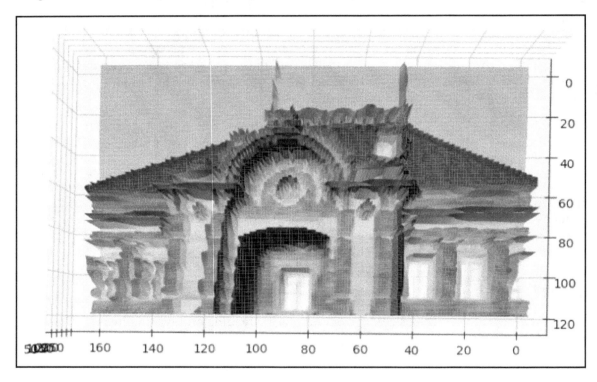

This is a top view, but on viewing sideways we can see the variation in the intensities that make up the image:

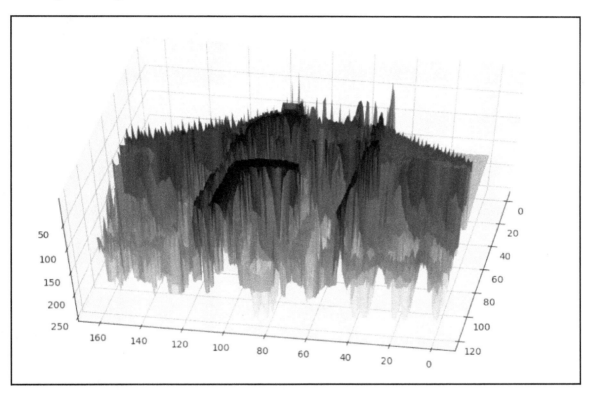

We can see that there are several peaks and image intensities that are not smooth. Let's apply *smoothing algorithm*, the details for which can be seen in Chapter 3, *Image Filtering and Transformations in OpenCV*:

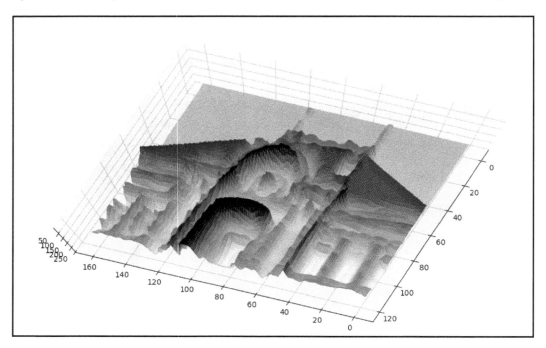

As we can see, pixel intensities form more continuous formations, even though there is no significant change in the object representation. The code to visualize this is as follows (the libraries required to visualize images are described in detail in the Chapter 2, *Libraries, Development Platforms, and Datasets,* separately):

```python
import numpy as np
import matplotlib.pyplot as plt
from mpl_toolkits.mplot3d import Axes3D
import cv2


# loads and read an image from path to file
img = cv2.imread('../figures/building_sm.png')

# convert the color to grayscale
gray = cv2.cvtColor(img, cv2.COLOR_BGR2GRAY)
# resize the image(optional)
gray = cv2.resize(gray, (160, 120))
```

```
# apply smoothing operation
gray = cv2.blur(gray,(3,3))

# create grid to plot using numpy
xx, yy = np.mgrid[0:gray.shape[0], 0:gray.shape[1]]

# create the figure
fig = plt.figure()
ax = fig.gca(projection='3d')
ax.plot_surface(xx, yy, gray ,rstride=1, cstride=1, cmap=plt.cm.gray,
        linewidth=1)
# show it
plt.show()
```

This code uses the following libraries: NumPy, OpenCV, and matplotlib.

In the further sections of this chapter we will see operations on images using their color properties. Please download the relevant images from the website to view them clearly.

Reading an image

An image, stored in digital format, consists of grid structure with each cell containing a value to represent image. In further sections, we will see different formats for images. For each format, the values represented in the grid cells will have different range of values.

To manipulate an image or use it for further processing, we need to load the image and use it as grid like structure. This is referred to as image input-output operations and we can use OpenCV library to read an image, as follows. Here, change the path to the image file according to use:

```
import cv2

# loads and read an image from path to file
img = cv2.imread('../figures/flower.png')

# displays previous image
cv2.imshow("Image",img)

# keeps the window open until a key is pressed
cv2.waitKey(0)

# clears all window buffers
cv2.destroyAllWindows()
```

The resulting image is shown in the following screenshot:

Here, we read the image in BGR color format where B is blue, G is green, and R is red. Each pixel in the output is collectively represented using the values of each of the colors. An example of the pixel location and its color values is shown in the previous figure bottom.

Image color conversions

An image is made up pixels and is usually visualized according to the value stored. There is also an additional property that makes different kinds of image. Each of the value stored in a pixel is linked to a fixed representation. For example, a pixel value of ten can represent gray intensity value ten or blue color intensity value 10 and so on. It is therefore important to understand different color types and their conversion. In this section, we will see color types and conversions using OpenCV:

- **Grayscale**: This is a simple one channel image with values ranging from 0 to 255 that represent the intensity of pixels. The previous image can be converted to grayscale, as follows:

```
import cv2

# loads and read an image from path to file
img = cv2.imread('../figures/flower.png')

# convert the color to grayscale
gray = cv2.cvtColor(img, cv2.COLOR_BGR2GRAY)

# displays previous image
cv2.imshow("Image",gray)

# keeps the window open until a key is pressed
cv2.waitKey(0)

# clears all window buffers
cv2.destroyAllWindows()
```

The resulting image is as shown in the following screenshot:

- **HSV and HLS**: These are another representation of color representing H is hue, S is saturation, V is value, and L is lightness. These are motivated by the human perception system. An example of image conversion for these is as follows:

```
# convert the color to hsv
hsv = cv2.cvtColor(img, cv2.COLOR_BGR2HSV)

# convert the color to hls
hls = cv2.cvtColor(img, cv2.COLOR_BGR2HLS)
```

This conversion is as shown in the following figure, where an input image read in BGR format is converted to each of the **HLS** (on left) and **HSV** (on right) color types:

• **LAB color space**: Denoted *L* for lightness, *A* for green-red colors, and B for blue-yellow colors, this consists of all perceivable colors. This is used to convert between one type of color space (for example, RGB) to others (such as CMYK) because of its device independence properties. On devices where the format is different to that of the image that is sent, the incoming image color space is first converted to LAB and then to the corresponding space available on the device. The output of converting an RGB image is as follows:

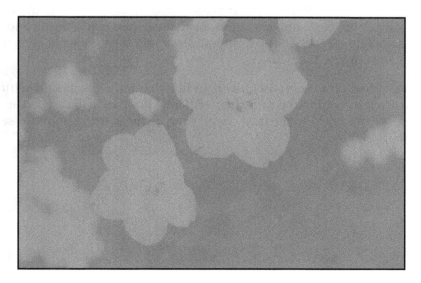

Computer vision research conferences

Some of the conferences to look for latest research and applications are as follows:

- **CVPR: Conference on Computer Vision and Pattern Recognition** is held every year and is one of the popular conferences with research papers ranging from both theory and application across a wide domain
- **ICCV: International Conference on Computer Vision** is another major conference held every other year attracting one of the best research papers
- **SIGGRAPH: Special Interest Group on Computer Graphics** and interactive techniques though more on computer graphics domain has several applications papers that utilizes computer vision techniques.

Other notable conferences include **Neural Information Processing Systems (NIPS)**, **International Conference on Machine Learning (ICML)**, **Asian Conference on Computer Vision (ACCV)**, **European Conference on Computer Vision (ECCV)**, and so on.

Summary

In this chapter, we saw a brief overview of computer vision with basic IO operations on images. Though it is a vast field, there are always exciting applications that can be built using computer vision techniques. This book tries to bridge the gap between theory and a practical approach to several of the popular algorithms. Further, in this book, we will begin with understanding more basic image operations that can perform filtering and transformations. Extending these basic techniques, we will then see what comprises of feature and how to compute them.

Following the introduction to computer vision in this chapter, we will start setting up libraries and an environment in the next chapter. These libraries will be used across the book. The datasets introduced in the next chapter can be the starting point for several algorithms further.

2
Libraries, Development Platform, and Datasets

In this chapter, we will be setting up a development environment to help run codes for the book as well as for generic development and also introduce various datasets for computer vision. Since there are several standard libraries which are used both for studying computer vision and in the industry for deployment, it becomes trivial to also use them in learning path. As we study the various sub-topics of computer vision in further chapters, we will be able to directly implement the codes introduced then rather than getting stuck in installations and other library dependencies.

This chapter is divided into two major sections:

- Firstly we will be setting up python based environment such Anaconda
- We will then setup OpenCV and various forms of its installations
- For deep learning, we will also setup Keras and TensorFlow

Libraries and installation

Before we begin, it is required that we install each library. There are two major methods of installing a library:

- We download the source code and build binaries by compiling the code
- We can directly download binaries and put them in relevant directories

While downloading pre-built binaries is a faster method, however, due to the difference of platforms or non-availability of binaries may force to build a library from source. If readers are using different OS then the mentioned in the following sections, they might come across such a situation. Once installed a library, it can be used with programs or other libraries.

Since it is crucial to have libraries that are not affected by other installations, we will be using Python-based environments in most of the book. This helps in keeping track of libraries installed and also separates different environment if we would like to have multiple. Here environment refers to installed libraries with particular versions and their dependencies.

For building a library from source, we will use `CMake` tool. The instructions to install are as shown in further sections. This helps in building cross-platform software by linking to relevant compilers on each platform as well as to their dependencies. This comes with GUI too but for convenience, we will be using command-line `cmake`.

For deep learning, which we will see later in this book, a GPU is highly recommended. To run our programs using GPUs, we need to install both CUDA and cuDNN binaries provided by Nvidia. Further details of installation for each of the platforms, such as Linux, Mac OS, or Windows, are available from Nvidia.

Let's begin by installing the required packages in order.

Installing Anaconda

The first thing we need to do is set up our Python environment such that rest of the libraries will be easily accessible through Python. Anaconda is a popular data science platform with a Python interface and is available here: `https://www.anaconda.com/`. It has `conda` as a package manager, which can install, delete, and manage versions of Python libraries while keeping it isolated from other Python environments. In this book, we will use `conda` from Anaconda. Let's go ahead and set this up.

First, download and install Anaconda:

- On Linux:

```
wget
https://repo.continuum.io/archive/Anaconda3-5.0.1-Linux-x86_64.sh
bash Anaconda3-5.0.1-MacOSX-x86_64.sh
```

- On macOS, `wget` is not directly available; use brew to install `wget`:

```
wget
https://repo.continuum.io/archive/Anaconda3-5.0.1-MacOSX-x86_64.sh
bash Anaconda3-5.0.1-MacOSX-x86_64.sh
```

This will install the Python libraries in the folder `$HOME/anaconda3`, since we are using Python 3. A Python 2 version is also available and the installation process is similar. To use Anaconda, the newly installed libraries need to be added in `$PATH`, this can be done every time a new shell is launched by running:

```
export PATH="$PATH_TO_ANACONDA3/anaconda3/bin:$PATH"
```

`$PATH_TO_ANACONDA3` is the location path to the `Anaconda3` folder. For more convenience, add this to `.bashrc` or `.bash_profile` depending on if you are using Linux or macOS respectively.

Once conda is installed, many other scientific packages will also be installed. Some of these packages are:

NumPy

NumPy package is used for performing operations on images as N-dimensional arrays. An example to create and transpose a two-dimensional array is as follows:

```
import numpy as np

A = [[1, 2],[3, 4]]

# transpose A
np.transpose(A)
```

Matplotlib

This is a popular Python package for plotting and displaying data and images. To use in Python, the scripts is as follows:

```
import matplotlib.pyplot as plt
```

If we want to plot inside Jupyter notebook, add the following command:

```
%matplotlib inline
```

An example function to display an image is as follows:

```
def plot_img(input_image):
    """
    Takes in image
    Plots image using matplotlib
    """
    plt.figure(figsize=(12,8))
    # change color channels order for matplotlib
    plt.imshow(input_image)

    # For easier view, turn off axis around image
    plt.axis('off')
    plt.show()
```

SciPy

This is a Python based scientific computing library and contains several advanced algorithms for optimization, linear algebra, signal processing, statistics, and so on.

An example to compute eigen values and eigen vectors of a two-dimensional array is as follows:

```
from scipy import linalg

A = [[5, 6], [7, 8]]
eig_vals, eig_vectors = linalg.eig(A)
```

Jupyter notebook

Jupyter notebook is popularly used for creating step by step live codes with visualizations and texts. In Chapter 3, *Image Filtering and Transformations in OpenCV* and Chapter 4, *What is a Feature?*, the codes for image filtering and feature extraction can be used with Jupyter notebook.

To launch a notebook server, run the following in shell:

```
jupyter notebook
```

This will start the browser and we can see the files inside the folder from where it is launched. After launching, click on **New** on top left side on the browser page and select the notebook with desired Python. A new tab in the browser will open with Python interpreter format.

Other packages such as scikit-learn, pandas, seaborn, and so on.

Installing OpenCV

OpenCV (available at `https://opencv.org/`) is the most popular computer vision open source library and can be installed on all major platforms including Linux, macOS, Windows, Android, iOS, and so on. It contains optimized code written in C++ and has binding for Python and Java. Considering the versatility of OpenCV, we will be using it to explain computer vision algorithms. Most of the code in this book is in Python, except for external repositories. OpenCV can be set up in two ways depending on how we will use it. We will begin with the easy way.

OpenCV Anaconda installation

Using Anaconda, which we installed in the previous section, OpenCV can be installed on both Linux and macOS as follows (this is OpenCV with only the Python library):

```
conda install -c conda-forge opencv
```

OpenCV build from source

Building OpenCV from source is quite a long process, depending on the hardware you are using:

- Requirements on Linux (here Ubuntu):

    ```
    sudo apt-get install build-essential
    sudo apt-get install cmake git libgtk2.0-dev pkg-config libavcodec-
    dev libavformat-dev libswscale-dev
    sudo apt-get install libtbb2 libtbb-dev libjpeg-dev libpng-dev
    libtiff-dev libjasper-dev libdc1394-22-dev
    ```

- Requirements on macOS:
    - Install CMake from `http://www.cmake.org/download/`

The following is an install script; copy the following snippet to install the `install.sh` file, and run `bash install.sh` to install OpenCV.

In the following code, replace `$PATH_TO_ANACONDA` with the absolute path to Anaconda, such as `/Users/mac`:

```
# download opencv
wget https://github.com/opencv/opencv/archive/3.3.0.zip
unzip 3.3.0.zip
mv opencv-3.3.0 opencv
rm -rf 3.3.0.zip


# install opencv
cd opencv
mkdir build && cd build
cmake -D -
DPYTHON_INCLUDE_DIR=$PATH_TO_ANACONDA/anaconda3/include/python3.6m/ \
    -DPYTHON_EXECUTABLE=$PATH_TO_ANACONDA/anaconda3/bin/python \
    -DPYTHON_PACKAGES_PATH=$PATH_TO_ANACONDA/anaconda3/lib/python3.6/site-
packages \
    -DINSTALL_PYTHON_EXAMPLES=ON \
    -DCMAKE_INSTALL_PREFIX=$PATH_TO_ANACONDA/anaconda3 \
    -DWITH_QT=ON \
    -DFORCE_VTK=ON \
    -DWITH_GDAL=ON \
    -DWITH_FFMPEG=ON \
    -DWITH_TBB=ON \
    -DWITH_XINE=ON \
    -DWITH_OPENCL=OFF \
    -DBUILD_EXAMPLES=ON ..

make -j4
make install
```

Since there are significant changes between OpenCV2 and OpenCV3, the code in this book is written using only OpenCV3.

In `OpenCV`, extra contributed modules are moved to a separate repository under the name `opencv_contrib`. In order to build `OpenCV` including with `opencv_contrib`, the steps are as follows:

- Download OpenCV as :

```
# download opencv
wget https://github.com/opencv/opencv/archive/3.3.0.zip
```

```
unzip 3.3.0.zip
mv opencv-3.3.0 opencv
rm -rf 3.3.0.zip
```

- Download the extra module here, and note the path to this folder:

```
# opencv contrib code
wget https://github.com/opencv/opencv_contrib/archive/3.3.0.zip
unzip 3.3.0.zip
mv opencv_contrib-3.3.0 opencv_contrib
rm -rf 3.3.0.zip
```

- Build a complete OpenCV again, as follows, where PATH_TO_CONTRIB is the path to the previously downloaded opencv_contrib path:

```
cd opencv
mkdir build && cd build
cmake -D -
DOPENCV_EXTRA_MODULES_PATH=$PATH_TO_CONTRIB/opencv_contrib/modules
\
    -
DPYTHON_INCLUDE_DIR=$PATH_TO_ANACONDA/anaconda3/include/python3.6m/
\
    -DPYTHON_EXECUTABLE=$PATH_TO_ANACONDA/anaconda3/bin/python \
    -
DPYTHON_PACKAGES_PATH=$PATH_TO_ANACONDA/anaconda3/lib/python3.6/sit
e-packages \
    -DINSTALL_PYTHON_EXAMPLES=ON \
    -DCMAKE_INSTALL_PREFIX=$PATH_TO_ANACONDA/anaconda3 \
    -DWITH_QT=ON \
    -DFORCE_VTK=ON \
    -DWITH_GDAL=ON \
    -DWITH_FFMPEG=ON \
    -DWITH_TBB=ON \
    -DWITH_XINE=ON \
    -DWITH_OPENCL=OFF \
    -DBUILD_EXAMPLES=ON ..

make -j4
make install
```

Here, we see that there are several options which are set on or off. The choice of these operations depends on the availability of the dependencies. These can be set to on if all of the dependencies are available.

Opencv FAQs

Though we saw an introductory OpenCV programs in previous chapter, we will see some more frequently used code snippets that will be used throughout this book.

- Let's begin with importing OpenCV and will print the version of OpenCV used:

```
import cv2
print(cv2.__version__)
```

- We can read an image from a file as:

```
img = cv2.imread('flower.png')
```

The previous snippet will decode an image stored in common formats such as `.jpg`, `.png`, `.jpeg`, `.tiff`, `.pgm`, and so on. using image codecs either installed with OpenCV or available on the platform. If there are no codecs available, then OpenCV will not be able to read image or write image to a file. So, it is necessary for the user to install codecs on a non-supported platforms such as embedded devices.

We can write an image to file as:

```
cv2.imwrite('image.png', img)
```

In writing a file also there is need for image codecs which are generally installed with OpenCV. We can write the image with file formats such as JPG, PNG, JPEG, TIFF, and so on.

Processing a video includes opening a video file and applying algorithms on each frame. We will first initialize the source of frames which can be a video file or an attached USB camera as:

```
# to use default usb camera set the value to 0
video_capture = cv2.VideoCapture(0)
```

Or we can also write it as follows:

```
# to use video file, set filename
video_capture = cv2.VideoCapture('video.avi')
```

Similar to image reading and writing, video reading will also require codecs which are installed with OpenCV or available from the OS. Once the source is setup we can continue processing each frame as:

```
while(True):
    # get each frame
```

```
ret, frame = video_capture.read()
# if no frame available then quit
if not ret:
    print("Frame not available")
    break
# show read frame in window
cv2.imshow('frame', frame)

# escape the loop on pressing 'q'
if cv2.waitKey(1) & 0xFF == ord('q'):
    break
```

Here `cv2.imshow` is to display image and `cv2.waitKey()` is time delay in the execution.

TensorFlow for deep learning

TensorFlow is one of the popular deep learning libraries available and has APIs for Python, C++, Java, and so on. In this book, we will use the Python API 1.4.0. Explaining TensorFlow in detail is beyond the scope of this book; the official documentation is a better starting place to get acquainted with it.

In order to install, we will use the `pip` based method, as follows:

```
pip install tensorflow=1.4.0
```

If there is GPU available with CUDA and cuDNN:

```
pip install tensorflow-gpu=1.4.0
```

For more information on TensorFlow and its use, please follow the tutorials here:

`https://www.tensorflow.org/get_started/get_started`.

Once installed, TensorFlow version can be checked by running:

```
python -c "import tensorflow as tf;print(tf.__version__)"
```

Keras for deep learning

Keras is a Python based API that uses TensorFlow, CNTK, or Theano as backend for deep learning. Due to its high level API and simplified abstraction, it has been quite popular in the deep learning community. We will be using this library to study CNNs. To install this, first install TensorFlow as described in previous section, and use the following:

```
pip install keras
```

There is no separate version for GPU. For installing specific versions of Keras, such as Version 2.1.2, use following:

```
pip install keras==2.1.2
```

The latest version of Keras at the time of writing this book is 2.1.2. To check the version of installed Keras, use:

```
python -c "import keras;print(keras.__version__)"
```

If TensorFlow is installed from previous sections, it will use it as backend.

To use Keras, one of the prerequisites is basic knowledge of deep learning. In this book, we will see it in `Chapter 5`, *Convolutional Neural Networks*.

Datasets

In computer vision, datasets play a key role in developing efficient applications. Also, now, with the availability of large open source datasets, it has become much easier to create best performing models for computer vision tasks. In this section, we will see several datasets for computer vision.

ImageNet

ImageNet is one of the largest annotated datasets for computer vision. The data is arranged according to a hierarchical order. There are 1,000 classes with 1.4 million images overall. Though the images are for non-commercial use, ImageNet is still one of the most popular datasets when it comes to learning computer vision. Especially in deep learning, the dataset is used to create image classification models due to availability of large number of varied images.

The following website provides links and resources to download image URLs or other attributes about images:

```
http://image-net.org/download
```

In this book, ImageNet is not used explicitly, but we will be using a pre-trained model on it. There is no requirement to download this dataset for this book.

MNIST

MNIST is a dataset for handwritten digits with the numbers 0-9 with 60,000 images of size 28 x 28 as the training set and 10,000 images of size 28 x 28 as the test set. This has become the go to dataset for starting machine learning or deep learning. It is provided in most of the frameworks and there is no need to download it separately. In Keras, this can be used as follows:

```python
from __future__ import print_function

from keras.datasets import mnist
import matplotlib.pyplot as plt

# Download and load dataset
(x_train, y_train), (x_test, y_test) = mnist.load_data()

# to know the size of data
print("Train data shape:", x_train.shape, "Test data shape:", x_test.shape)

# plot sample image
idx = 0
print("Label:",y_train[idx])
plt.imshow(x_train[idx], cmap='gray')
plt.axis('off')
plt.show()
```

Some of the sample images from this dataset are as shown in the following figure:

CIFAR-10

Though MNIST is one of the easiest datasets to get started, the lack of color images makes it less appealing for tasks that require a colored dataset. A slight more complex dataset is CIFAR-10 by Alex and others[1], which consists of 10 categories of images with 60,000 training images and 10,000 test images, uniformly from each category. The size of each image is 32 x 32 and each has three color channels. This dataset can also be easily loaded in Keras, as follows:

```
from __future__ import print_function

from keras.datasets import cifar10
import matplotlib.pyplot as plt

# Download and load dataset
(x_train, y_train), (x_test, y_test) = cifar10.load_data()
labels = ['airplane', 'automobile', 'bird', 'cat', 'deer', 'dog', 'frog',
'horse', 'ship', 'truck']
# to know the size of data
print("Train data shape:", x_train.shape, "Test data shape:", x_test.shape)

# plot sample image
idx = 1500
print("Label:",labels[y_train[idx][0]])
plt.imshow(x_train[idx])
plt.axis('off')
plt.show()
```

The labels, in order, are: airplane, automobile, bird, cat, deer, dog, frog, horse, ship, and truck.

Pascal VOC

As previous datasets like MNIST and CIFAR are limited in representation, we cannot use them for tasks like people detection or segmentation. Pascal VOC[4] has gained in popularity for such tasks as one of the major datasets for object recognition. During 2005-2012, there were competitions conducted that used this dataset and achieved the best possible accuracy on test data. The dataset is also usually referred to by year; for example, VOC2012 refers to the dataset available for the 2012 competition. In VOC2012, there are three competition categories. The first is the classification and detection dataset, which has 20 categories of objects along with rectangular region annotations around the objects. The second category is Segmentation with instance boundaries around objects. The third competition category is for action recognition from images.

This dataset can be downloaded from the following link:

`http://host.robots.ox.ac.uk/pascal/VOC/voc2012/index.html`.

In this dataset, a sample annotation file (in XML format) for an image is in the following code, where the tags represent properties of that field:

```
<annotation>
  <folder>VOC2012</folder>
  <filename>2007_000033.jpg</filename>
  <source>
    <database>The VOC2007 Database</database>
    <annotation>PASCAL VOC2007</annotation>
    <image>flickr</image>
  </source>
  <size>
    <width>500</width>
    <height>366</height>
    <depth>3</depth>
  </size>
  <segmented>1</segmented>
  <object>
    <name>aeroplane</name>
    <pose>Unspecified</pose>
    <truncated>0</truncated>
    <difficult>0</difficult>
    <bndbox>
      <xmin>9</xmin>
      <ymin>107</ymin>
      <xmax>499</xmax>
      <ymax>263</ymax>
    </bndbox>
  </object>
  <object>
    <name>aeroplane</name>
    <pose>Left</pose>
    <truncated>0</truncated>
    <difficult>0</difficult>
    <bndbox>
      <xmin>421</xmin>
      <ymin>200</ymin>
      <xmax>482</xmax>
      <ymax>226</ymax>
    </bndbox>
  </object>
  <object>
    <name>aeroplane</name>
```

```
      <pose>Left</pose>
      <truncated>1</truncated>
      <difficult>0</difficult>
      <bndbox>
         <xmin>325</xmin>
         <ymin>188</ymin>
         <xmax>411</xmax>
         <ymax&amp;gt;223</ymax>
      </bndbox>
   </object>
</annotation>
```

The corresponding image is as shown in the following figure:

The available categories in this dataset are aeroplane, bicycle, boat, bottle, bus, car, cat, chair, cow, dining table, dog, horse, motorbike, person, potted plant, sheep, train, and TV.

The number of categories is, however, limited. In the next section, we will see a more elaborate dataset with 80 categories. Having a higher number of generic object categories will help in creating applications that can be used easily in more generic scenarios.

MSCOCO

COCO[2] refers to a common object in context and is a dataset for object recognition, with 80 categories and 330K images. After Pascal VOC'12, this became a popular benchmark for training and evaluating the system. The dataset can be downloaded from `http://cocodataset.org/#download`.

In order to read the data and use it for applications, there is an API available at `https://github.com/cocodataset/cocoapi` which needs to be downloaded. To get started, we can use the API provided, as follows:

```
git clone https://github.com/cocodataset/cocoapi.git
cd cocoapi/PythonAPI
make
```

This will install the Python API to read the `coco` dataset.

Many models available online for object detection or image segmentation are first trained on this dataset. If we have specific data that has different object categories than in the MSCOCO dataset, a more common approach that we will see in `Chapter 5`, *Convolution Neural Networks* and in `Chapter 6`, *Feature- Based Object Detection*, is to first train a model on an MSCOCO dataset and use a part of the trained model and re-train on a new dataset.

TUM RGB-D dataset

While previous datasets were used for object recognition, this dataset is used to understand the geometry of a scene. The RGB-D dataset[3] has been popular in SLAM research and was a benchmark for comparison too. Here, RGB-D refers to a dataset with both **RGB** (color) images and **Depth** images. The depth here refers to distance of pixel from camera and are taken using a depth camera. Since there is also depth information available, this dataset can also be used to evaluate depth based SLAM algorithms and three-dimensional reconstructions from RGB image and its corresponding depth image.

To download this dataset, visit `https://vision.in.tum.de/data/datasets/rgbd-dataset/download` and choose the type of sequence to use.

Summary

In this chapter, we learned how to install the different library files of Python, Keras, and TensorFlow. In order to use several code snippets in further chapters, these libraries will be sufficient. We also had a look at different datasets like ImageNet, MNIST, CIFAR-10, MSCOCO and TUM RGBD datasets. These datasets are the backbone for computer vision applications since the ability of several software that we develop directly depends on the availability of these datasets.

In next chapter, we will begin with more in-depth image analysis by introducing different types of filters and also learn transformations on image such as translation, rotation or affine.

References

- Krizhevsky, Alex, and Geoffrey Hinton. *Learning multiple layers of features from tiny images*. (2009).
- Lin, Tsung-Yi, Michael Maire, Serge Belongie, James Hays, Pietro Perona, Deva Ramanan, Piotr Dollár, and C. Lawrence Zitnick. *Microsoft coco: Common objects in context*. In European conference on computer vision, pp. 740-755. Springer, Cham, 2014.
- Sturm, Jürgen, Nikolas Engelhard, Felix Endres, Wolfram Burgard, and Daniel Cremers. *A benchmark for the evaluation of RGB-D SLAM systems*. In Intelligent Robots and Systems (IROS), 2012 IEEE/RSJ International Conference on, pp. 573-580. IEEE, 2012.
- Everingham Mark, Luc Van Gool, Christopher KI Williams, John Winn, and Andrew Zisserman. *The pascal visual object classes (voc) challenge*. International journal of computer vision 88, no. 2 (2010): 303-338.

3

Image Filtering and Transformations in OpenCV

In this chapter, you will learn the basic building blocks for computer vision applications. We are already familiar with digital cameras and smartphone devices with auto image enhancement or color adjustments to make our photographs more pleasing. The techniques behind these originated long ago and have come through several iterations to become better and faster. Many of the techniques explained in this chapter also become major preprocessing techniques for object detection and object classification tasks introduced later. Hence, it is very important to study these techniques and understand their applications.

You will study the basis for these applications with several techniques for filtering an image linearly as well as non-linearly.

Later in the chapter, you will also study transformation techniques and downsampling techniques. A code is provided together with explanations and sample output. Readers are encouraged to write the code and experiment with changing parameters to understand several concepts. There are several colored image results in this chapter, for an effective understanding download the images from book's website.

In this chapter, we will learn the following topics:

- Datasets and libraries required
- Image manipulation
- Introduction to filters
- Transformations on an image
- Image pyramids

Datasets and libraries required

We will be using a sample image for most of this task. However, you can try the code with any other image or also use a webcam to see live results. The libraries used in this chapter are OpenCV, NumPy, and matplotlib. Even if you are not acquainted with libraries, you can still understand the code and implement them. There are also remarks for special cases when using a Jupyter notebook for the code written here:

```
import numpy as np
import matplotlib.pyplot as plt
import cv2
# With jupyter notebook uncomment below line
# %matplotlib inline
# This plots figures inside the notebook
```

The sample image used in this chapter can be loaded as follows:

```
# read an image
img = cv2.imread('flower.png')
```

This image can be plotted either using OpenCV or matplotlib libraries. We will be using matplotlib for the majority of plots as this will be beneficial in plotting other kinds of data as well in later chapters. A plotting function for a colored image read in OpenCV is defined as follows:

```
def plot_cv_img(input_image):
    """
    Converts an image from BGR to RGB and plots
    """
    # change color channels order for matplotlib
    plt.imshow(cv2.cvtColor(input_image, cv2.COLOR_BGR2RGB))

    # For easier view, turn off axis around image
    plt.axis('off')
    plt.show()
```

The previously read image can be plotted as follows:

The image in Python is a NumPy array, so all of the array operations are still valid in the image. For example, you can crop an image by using array slicing:

```
plot_cv_img(img[100:400, 100:400])
```

This results in the following:

Image manipulation

As explained in previous chapters, an image in the digital domain, such as on a computer, is made up of a grid-like structure with each grid cell termed a **pixel**. These pixels store a value representing information about the image. For a simple grayscale image, these pixels store an integer with range [0, 255]. Changing these pixel values also changes the image. One of the basic image manipulation techniques is modifying pixel values.

Let's start by displaying what is inside an image at pixel level. For simplicity, we will do analysis on a grayscale image:

```
# read an image
img = cv2.imread('gray_flower.png')
```

The earlier code reads a grayscale image from a file, in this case the image is in PNG format. We can also convert from one type of image color format to another. In this case, to convert a colored image to grayscale, OpenCV provides functions as follows:

```
# converts rgb image to grayscale
gray_output = cv2.cvtColor(color_input, cv2.COLOR_BGR2GRAY)
```

The previously shown code for displaying an image takes only a colored image as input, so to display a grayscale image there needs to be some modification:

```
def plot_cv_img(input_image,is_gray=False):
    """
    Takes in image with flag showing, if gray or not
    Plots image using matplotlib
    """
    # change color channels order for matplotlib
    if not is_gray:
        plt.imshow(cv2.cvtColor(input_image, cv2.COLOR_BGR2RGB))
    else:
        plt.imshow(input_image, cmap='gray')

    # For easier view, turn off axis around image
    plt.axis('off')
    plt.show()
```

The output of the previous code is as follows:

We can display a small patch from this image as follows, that shows pixel values:

```
# read the image
flower = cv2.imread('../figures/flower.png')

# convert to gray scale
gray_flower = cv2.cvtColor(flower, cv2.COLOR_BGR2GRAY)

# take out a patch of pixels
patch_gray = gray_flower[250:260, 250:260]

#plot the patch as well as print the values
plot_cv_img(patch_gray, is_gray=True)
print(patch_gray)
```

This will produce an image of the patch and prints out the value extracted in that patch:

Corresponding values are as follows, the lower values represent more darker regions:

```
[[142 147 150 154 164 113  39  40  39  38]
 [146 145 148 152 156  78  42  41  40  40]
 [147 148 147 147 143  62  42  42  44  44]
 [155 148 147 145 142  91  42  44  43  44]
 [156 154 149 147 143 113  43  42  42  48]
 [155 157 152 149 149 133  68  45  47  50]
 [155 154 155 150 152 145  94  48  48  48]
 [152 151 153 151 152 146 106  51  50  47]
 [155 157 152 150 153 145 112  50  49  49]
 [156 154 152 151 149 147 115  49  52  52]]
```

These are the intensities for a pixel and is represented as a two-dimensional array. The range of each pixel value is 0-255. In order to modify image, we change these pixel values. A simple filtering for images is applying point operation targeted to multiply and add constants to each pixel values. We will see this type of filters in detail in the next section.

In this section, we saw basic IO extending our discussion from Chapter 1, *A Fast Introduction to Computer Vision*. In further section, we will see how to modify these using filters which are used in image editing applications on smartphones, desktops and even on social media applications.

Introduction to filters

Filters are operations on an image to modify them so that they are usable for other computer vision tasks or to give us required information. These perform various functions such as removing noise from an image, extracting edges in an image, blurring an image, removing unwanted objects etc. We will see their implementations and understand the results.

Filtering techniques are necessary because there are several factors that may lead to noise in an image or undesired information in an image. Taking a picture in sunlight, induces lots of bright and dark areas in the image or an improper environment like night time, the image captured by a camera may contain a lot of noise. Also, in cases of unwanted objects or colors in an image, these are also considered noise.

An example of salt and pepper noise looks like the following:

The preceding image can be easily generated using OpenCV as follows:

```
# initialize noise image with zeros
noise = np.zeros((400, 600))

# fill the image with random numbers in given range
cv2.randu(noise, 0, 256)
```

Let's add weighted noise to a grayscale image (on the left) so the resulting image will look like the one on the right:

The code for this is as follows:

```
# add noise to existing image
noisy_gray = gray + np.array(0.2*noise, dtype=np.int)
```

Here, 0.2 is used as parameter, increase or decrease the value to create different intensity noise.

In several applications, noise plays an important role in improving a system's capabilities, especially when we will use Deep Learning based models in the upcoming chapters. It is quite crucial for several applications, to know how robust the application is against noise becomes very important. As an example, we would want the model designed for applications like image classification to work with noisy images as well, hence noise is deliberately added in the images to test the application precision.

Linear filters

To begin with, the simplest kind of filter is a point operator, where each pixel value is multiplied by a scalar value. This operation can be written as follows:

$$g(i, j) = K \times f(i, j)$$

Here:

- The input image is F and the value of pixel at *(i,j)* is denoted as *f(i,j)*
- The output image is G and the value of pixel at *(i,j)* is denoted as *g(i,j)*
- *K* is scalar constant

Such an operation on an image is termed a **linear filter**. There are many more kinds of linear filters which you will be reading about further in this section. In addition to multiplication by a scalar value, each pixel can also be increased or decreased by a constant value. So overall point operation can be written as follows:

$$g(i, j) = K \times f(i, j) + L$$

This operation can be applied both to grayscale images and RGB images. For RGB images, each channel will be modified with this operation separately. The following is the result of varying both *K* and *L*. The first image is input on the left. In the second image, K=0.5 and L=0.0, while in the third image, K is set to 1.0 and L is 10. For the final image on the right, K=0.7 and L=25. As you can see, varying *K* changes the brightness of the image and varying *L* changes the contrast of the image:

This image can be generated with the following code:

```
import numpy as np
import matplotlib.pyplot as plt
import cv2

def point_operation(img, K, L):
    """
    Applies point operation to given grayscale image
    """
    img = np.asarray(img, dtype=np.float)
    img = img*K + L
    # clip pixel values
    img[img > 255] = 255
    img[img < 0] = 0
    return np.asarray(img, dtype = np.int)
```

```
def main():
    # read an image
    img = cv2.imread('../figures/flower.png')
    gray = cv2.cvtColor(img, cv2.COLOR_BGR2GRAY)
    # k = 0.5, l = 0
    out1 = point_operation(gray, 0.5, 0)

    # k = 1., l = 10
    out2 = point_operation(gray, 1., 10)

    # k = 0.8, l = 15
    out3 = point_operation(gray, 0.7, 25)
    res = np.hstack([gray,out1, out2, out3])
    plt.imshow(res, cmap='gray')
    plt.axis('off')

    plt.show()


if __name__ == '__main__':
    main()
```

2D linear filters

While the preceding filter is a point-based filter, image pixels have information around the pixel as well. In the previous image of the flower, the pixel values in the petal are all yellow. If we choose a pixel of the petal and move around, the values will be quite close. This gives some more information about the image. To extract this information in filtering, there are several neighborhood filters.

In neighborhood filters, there is a kernel matrix which captures local region information around a pixel. To explain these filters, let's start with an input image, as follows:

0	1	1	0
0	0	0	1
0	0	1	0
0	1	1	1

This is a simple binary image of the number 2. To get certain information from this image, we can directly use all the pixel values. But instead, to simplify, we can apply filters on this. We define a matrix smaller than the given image which operates in the neighborhood of a target pixel. This matrix is termed **kernel**; an example is given as follows:

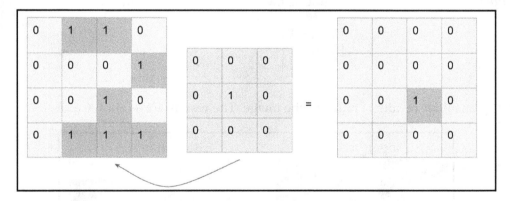

The operation is defined first by superimposing the kernel matrix on the original image, then taking the product of the corresponding pixels and returning a summation of all the products. In the following figure, the lower 3 x 3 area in the original image is superimposed with the given kernel matrix and the corresponding pixel values from the kernel and image are multiplied. The resulting image is shown on the right and is the summation of all the previous pixel products:

This operation is repeated by sliding the kernel along image rows and then image columns. This can be implemented as in following code. We will see the effects of applying this on an image in coming sections:

```
# design a kernel matrix, here is uniform 5x5
kernel = np.ones((5,5),np.float32)/25

# apply on the input image, here grayscale  input
dst = cv2.filter2D(gray,-1,kernel)
```

However, as you can see previously, the corner pixel will have a drastic impact and results in a smaller image because the kernel, while overlapping, will be outside the image region. This causes a black region, or holes, along with the boundary of an image. To rectify this, there are some common techniques used:

- Padding the corners with constant values maybe 0 or 255, by default OpenCV will use this.
- Mirroring the pixel along the edge to the external area
- Creating a pattern of pixels around the image

The choice of these will depend on the task at hand. In common cases, padding will be able to generate satisfactory results.

The effect of the kernel is most crucial as changing these values changes the output significantly. We will first see simple kernel-based filters and also see their effects on the output when changing the size.

Box filters

This filter averages out the pixel value as the kernel matrix is denoted as follows:

$$\frac{1}{9} \begin{bmatrix} 1 & 1 & 1 \\ 1 & 1 & 1 \\ 1 & 1 & 1 \end{bmatrix}$$

Applying this filter results in blurring the image. The results are as shown as follows:

In frequency domain analysis of the image, this filter is a low pass filter. The frequency domain analysis is done using Fourier transformation of the image, which is beyond the scope of this introduction. We can see on changing the kernel size, the image gets more and more blurred:

As we increase the size of the kernel, we can observe that resulting image gets more blurred. This is due to averaging out of peak values in the small neighborhood where the kernel is applied. The result for applying kernel of size 20 x 20 can be seen in the following image:

However, if we use a very small filter of size (3, 3) there is negligible effect on the output, due to the fact that the kernel size is quite small compared to the photo size. In most applications, kernel size is heuristically set according to image size:

The complete code to generate box filtered photos is as follows:

```
def plot_cv_img(input_image, output_image):
    """
    Converts an image from BGR to RGB and plots
    """

    fig, ax = plt.subplots(nrows=1, ncols=2)

    ax[0].imshow(cv2.cvtColor(input_image, cv2.COLOR_BGR2RGB))
    ax[0].set_title('Input Image')
    ax[0].axis('off')
    ax[1].imshow(cv2.cvtColor(output_image, cv2.COLOR_BGR2RGB))
    ax[1].set_title('Box Filter (5,5)')
    ax[1].axis('off')
    plt.show()

def main():
    # read an image
    img = cv2.imread('../figures/flower.png')
    # To try different kernel, change size here.
    kernel_size = (5,5)
    # opencv has implementation for kernel based box blurring
    blur = cv2.blur(img,kernel_size)

    # Do plot
    plot_cv_img(img, blur)

if __name__ == '__main__':
    main()
```

Properties of linear filters

Several computer vision applications are composed of step by step transformations of an input photo to output. This is easily done due to several properties associated with a common type of filters, that is, linear filters:

- The linear filters are commutative such that we can perform multiplication operations on filters in any order and the result still remains the same:

$$a * b = b * a$$

- They are associative in nature, which means the order of applying the filter does not effect the outcome:

$$(a * b) * c = a * (b * c)$$

- Even in cases of summing two filters, we can perform the first summation and then apply the filter, or we can also individually apply the filter and then sum the results. The overall outcome still remains the same:

$$b = (k+l) * a$$

- Applying a scaling factor to one filter and multiplying to another filter is equivalent to first multiplying both filters and then applying scaling factor

These properties play a significant role later, when we look at computer vision tasks such as object detection, segmentation, and so on. A suitable combination of these filters enhances the quality of information extraction and as a result, improves the accuracy.

Non-linear filters

While in many cases linear filters are sufficient to get the required results, in several other use cases performance can be significantly increased with the use of non-linear filters. As the name suggests, these filters are composed of more complex operations, have some kind of non-linearity, and as a result these filters do not follow some or all of the properties of linear filters.

We will understand these filters with implementations.

Smoothing a photo

Applying a box filter with hard edges doesn't result in a smooth blur on the output photo.

To improve this, the filter can be made smoother around the edges. One of the popular such filters is a **Gaussian filter**. This is a non-linear filter which enhances the effect of the center pixel and gradually reduces the effects as the pixel gets farther from the center. Mathematically, a Gaussian function is given as:

$$f(x) = \frac{1}{\sigma\sqrt{2\pi}} \exp(\frac{(x - \mu)^2}{2\sigma^2})$$

where μ is mean and σ is variance.

An example kernel matrix for this kind of filter in a two-dimensional discrete domain is given as follows:

$$\frac{1}{256} \begin{bmatrix} 1 & 4 & 6 & 4 & 1 \\ 4 & 16 & 24 & 16 & 4 \\ 6 & 24 & 36 & 24 & 6 \\ 4 & 16 & 24 & 16 & 4 \\ 1 & 4 & 6 & 4 & 1 \end{bmatrix}$$

This two-dimensional array is used in normalized form and effect of this filter also depends on its width by changing the kernel width has varying effects on the output as discussed in further section. Applying Gaussian kernel as filter removes high-frequency components which results in removing strong edges and hence a blurred photo:

While this filter performs better blurring than a box filter, the implementation is also quite simple with OpenCV:

```python
def plot_cv_img(input_image, output_image):
    """
    Converts an image from BGR to RGB and plots
    """
    fig, ax = plt.subplots(nrows=1, ncols=2)
    ax[0].imshow(cv2.cvtColor(input_image, cv2.COLOR_BGR2RGB))
    ax[0].set_title('Input Image')
    ax[0].axis('off')
    ax[1].imshow(cv2.cvtColor(output_image, cv2.COLOR_BGR2RGB))
    ax[1].set_title('Gaussian Blurred')
    ax[1].axis('off')
    plt.show()

def main():
    # read an image
    img = cv2.imread('../figures/flower.png')
    # apply gaussian blur,
    # kernel of size 5x5,
    # change here for other sizes
    kernel_size = (5,5)
    # sigma values are same in both direction
    blur = cv2.GaussianBlur(img, (5,5),0)
    plot_cv_img(img, blur)

if __name__ == '__main__':
    main()
```

Histogram equalization

The basic point operations, to change the brightness and contrast, help in improving photo quality but require manual tuning. Using histogram equalization technique, these can be found algorithmically and create a better-looking photo. Intuitively, this method tries to set the brightest pixels to white and the darker pixels to black. The remaining pixel values are similarly rescaled. This rescaling is performed by transforming original intensity distribution to capture all intensity distribution. An example of this equalization is as following:

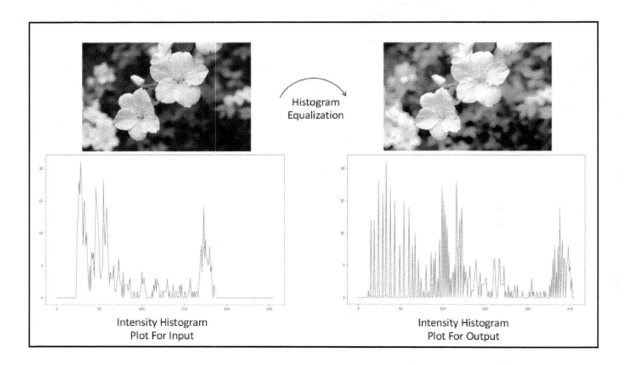

The preceding image is an example of histogram equalization. On the right is the output and, as you can see, the contrast is increased significantly. The input histogram is shown in the bottom figure on the left and it can be observed that not all the colors are observed in the image. After applying equalization, resulting histogram plot is as shown on the right bottom figure. To visualize the results of equalization in the image, the input and results are stacked together in following figure:

Code for the preceding photos is as follows:

```
def plot_gray(input_image, output_image):
    """
    Converts an image from BGR to RGB and plots
    """
    # change color channels order for matplotlib
    fig, ax = plt.subplots(nrows=1, ncols=2)

    ax[0].imshow(input_image, cmap='gray')
    ax[0].set_title('Input Image')
    ax[0].axis('off')
    ax[1].imshow(output_image, cmap='gray')
    ax[1].set_title('Histogram Equalized ')
    ax[1].axis('off')
    plt.savefig('../figures/03_histogram_equalized.png')

    plt.show()

def main():
    # read an image
    img = cv2.imread('../figures/flower.png')
    # grayscale image is used for equalization
    gray = cv2.cvtColor(img, cv2.COLOR_BGR2GRAY)
```

```
        # following function performs equalization on input image
        equ = cv2.equalizeHist(gray)
        # for visualizing input and output side by side
        plot_gray(gray, equ)
if __name__ == '__main__':
        main()
```

Median filter

This filter uses the same technique of neighborhood filtering; the key technique in this is the use of a median value. As such, the filter is non-linear. It is quite useful in removing sharp noise such as salt and pepper.

Instead of using a product or sum of neighborhood pixel values, this filter computes a median value of the region. This results in the removal of random peak values in the region, which can be due to noise like salt and pepper noise. This is further shown in the following figure with different kernel size used to create output.

In this image first input is added with channel wise random noise as:

```
# read the image
flower = cv2.imread('../figures/flower.png')

# initialize noise image with zeros
noise = np.zeros(flower.shape[:2])

# fill the image with random numbers in given range
cv2.randu(noise, 0, 256)

# add noise to existing image, apply channel wise
noise_factor = 0.1
noisy_flower = np.zeros(flower.shape)
for i in range(flower.shape[2]):
    noisy_flower[:,:,i] = flower[:,:,i] + np.array(noise_factor*noise,
dtype=np.int)

# convert data type for use
noisy_flower = np.asarray(noisy_flower, dtype=np.uint8)
```

The created noisy image is used for median filtering as:

```
# apply median filter of kernel size 5
kernel_5 = 5
median_5 = cv2.medianBlur(noisy_flower,kernel_5)


# apply median filter of kernel size 3
kernel_3 = 3
median_3 = cv2.medianBlur(noisy_flower,kernel_3)
```

In the following photo, you can see the resulting photo after varying the kernel size (indicated in brackets). The rightmost photo is the smoothest of them all:

The most common application for median blur is in smartphone application which filters input image and adds additional artifacts to add artistic effects.

The code to generate the preceding photograph is as follows:

```
def plot_cv_img(input_image, output_image1, output_image2, output_image3):
    """
    Converts an image from BGR to RGB and plots
    """

    fig, ax = plt.subplots(nrows=1, ncols=4)

    ax[0].imshow(cv2.cvtColor(input_image, cv2.COLOR_BGR2RGB))
    ax[0].set_title('Input Image')
    ax[0].axis('off')
    ax[1].imshow(cv2.cvtColor(output_image1, cv2.COLOR_BGR2RGB))
    ax[1].set_title('Median Filter (3,3)')
    ax[1].axis('off')

    ax[2].imshow(cv2.cvtColor(output_image2, cv2.COLOR_BGR2RGB))
    ax[2].set_title('Median Filter (5,5)')
    ax[2].axis('off')

    ax[3].imshow(cv2.cvtColor(output_image3, cv2.COLOR_BGR2RGB))
    ax[3].set_title('Median Filter (7,7)')
```

```
        ax[3].axis('off')
        plt.show()

def main():
    # read an image
    img = cv2.imread('../figures/flower.png')

    # compute median filtered image varying kernel size
    median1 = cv2.medianBlur(img,3)
    median2 = cv2.medianBlur(img,5)
    median3 = cv2.medianBlur(img,7)
    # Do plot
    plot_cv_img(img, median1, median2, median3)

if __name__ == '__main__':
    main()
```

Image gradients

These are more *edge detectors* or sharp changes in a photograph. Image gradients widely used in object detection and segmentation tasks. In this section, we will look at how to compute image gradients. First, the image derivative is applying the kernel matrix which computes the change in a direction.

The Sobel filter is one such filter and kernel in the x direction is given as follows:

$$\frac{1}{8}\begin{bmatrix} -1 & 0 & 1 \\ -2 & 0 & 2 \\ -1 & 0 & 1 \end{bmatrix}$$

Here, in the y direction:

$$\frac{1}{8}\begin{bmatrix} 1 & 2 & 1 \\ 0 & 0 & 0 \\ -1 & -2 & -1 \end{bmatrix}$$

This is applied in a similar fashion to the linear box filter by computing values on a superimposed kernel with the photo. The filter is then shifted along the image to compute all values. Following is some example results, where X and Y denote the direction of the Sobel kernel:

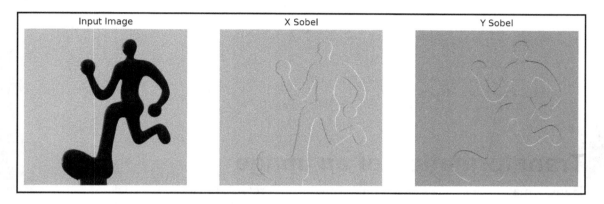

This is also termed as an image derivative with respect to given direction(here X or Y). The lighter resulting photographs (middle and right) are positive gradients, while the darker regions denote negative and gray is zero.

While Sobel filters correspond to first order derivatives of a photo, the Laplacian filter gives a second-order derivative of a photo. The Laplacian filter is also applied in a similar way to Sobel:

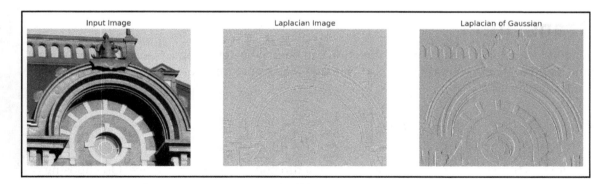

The code to get Sobel and Laplacian filters is as follows:

```
# sobel
x_sobel = cv2.Sobel(img,cv2.CV_64F,1,0,ksize=5)
y_sobel = cv2.Sobel(img,cv2.CV_64F,0,1,ksize=5)

# laplacian
lapl = cv2.Laplacian(img,cv2.CV_64F, ksize=5)

# gaussian blur
blur = cv2.GaussianBlur(img,(5,5),0)
# laplacian of gaussian
log = cv2.Laplacian(blur,cv2.CV_64F, ksize=5)
```

Transformation of an image

Transformation operations on an image are usually referred to as geometric transformations, applied on a photo. There are several other kinds of transformations as well but in this section we will refer to geometric transformations. These consist of, but are not limited to, shifting an image, rotating an image along an axis, or projecting it onto different planes.

At the core of transformation is a matrix multiplication of our image. We will look at different components of this matrix and the resulting image.

Translation

Displacement of an image in any direction can be done by creating a transformation matrix and applying the transformation to our image. The transformation matrix for translation only is given as:

$$T = \begin{bmatrix} 0 & 1 & t_x \\ 1 & 0 & ty \end{bmatrix}$$

where t_x is translation in x direction and t_y in y direction in image reference. On choosing different values of translation matrix, results are shown as follows:

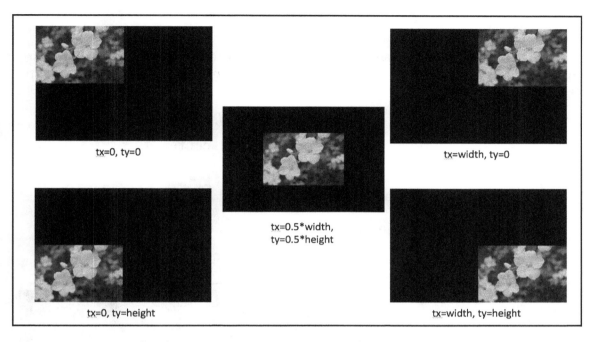

In the previous figure, output is images are larger than the input image to show the effects of translation otherwise only visible region of images which are inside the original image size will be shown.

Code for creating this translation is given as follows, here change the values of tx and ty to generate different translations:

```
# input shape
w, h = flower.shape[1], flower.shape[0]

# create translation matrix
tx = w/2 # half of width
ty = h/2 # half of height
translation_matrix = np.float32([[1,0,tx],
                                 [0,1,ty]])

# apply translation operation using warp affine function.
output_size = (w*2,h*2)
translated_flower = cv2.warpAffine(flower, translation_matrix, output_size)
```

Rotation

Similar to translation, rotating an image is also possible by creating a transformation matrix. Instead of creating translation matrix, in `OpenCV`, given a rotation angle θ, a rotation matrix is created of the form:

$$\begin{bmatrix} \alpha & \beta & (1-\alpha).\,center_x - \beta.\,center_y \\ -\beta & \alpha & \beta.\,center_x - (1-\alpha).\,center_y \end{bmatrix}$$

where,

$$\alpha = scale.\,cos\theta$$
$$\beta = scale.\,sin\theta$$

An example of applying result is as follows:

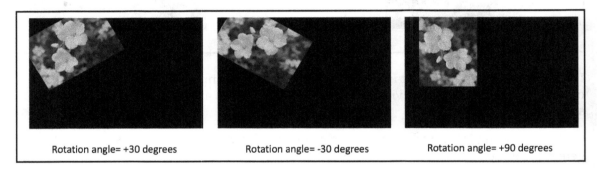

| Rotation angle= +30 degrees | Rotation angle= -30 degrees | Rotation angle= +90 degrees |

For the previous screenshot, the code is as follows:

```
# input shape
w, h = flower.shape[1], flower.shape[0]

# create rotation matrix
rot_angle = 90 # in degrees
scale = 1 # keep the size same
rotation_matrix = cv2.getRotationMatrix2D((w/2,h/2),rot_angle,1)

# apply rotation using warpAffine
output_size = (w*2,h*2)
rotated_flower = cv2.warpAffine(flower,rotation_matrix,output_size)
```

Similarly, transformations also can be done by combining both rotation and translation with scaling and as a result, the angle between the lines will be preserved.

Affine transform

With an Affine transform, only parallel lines will be preserved in the output. An example output image is as follows:

The code for the preceding image is as follows:

```
# create transformation matrix form preselected points
pts1 = np.float32([[50,50],[200,50],[50,200]])
pts2 = np.float32([[10,100],[200,50],[100,250]])

affine_tr = cv2.getAffineTransform(pts1,pts2)
transformed = cv2.warpAffine(img, affine_tr,
(img.shape[1]*2,img.shape[0]*2))
```

Image pyramids

Pyramids refer to rescaling a photograph either increasing the resolution or decreasing it. These are often used to increase the computation efficiency of computer vision algorithms such as image matching in a huge database. In such cases, image matching is computed on a downsampled image and later on the search is iteratively refined for a higher resolution of the image.

The downsampling and upsampling often depend on the pixel selection process. One of the simplest processes is selecting alternative rows and column pixel values to create a downsampled version of the photo as follows:

However, if we try to upsample from the rightmost picture in the previous figure, the results look as follows:

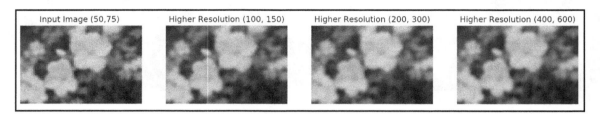

It can easily be seen that the rightmost picture above is not the same as the original one that we started with. This is due to the fact that we lose information during downsampling and hence the image cannot be recreated in the same way as the original one. In OpenCV, there is also blurring of input image before downsampling or upsampling. This also further makes it harder to keep the resolution intact.

The codes for downsampling is as follow:

```
# downsample image by halving both width and height
# input:(h, w) --> output:(h/2, w/2)
lower_resolution_img = cv2.pyrDown(img)
```

And for upsampling an image to twice its height and width sizes as:

```
# Upsamples image by doubling both width and height
# input:(h, w) --> output:(h*2, w*2)
higher_resolution_img = cv2.pyrUp(img)
```

Summary

In this chapter, we started with initial image analysis by applying various manipulation. We began discussion with point filters and extending to more complex linear as well as non linear filters. We saw the visualization of results on varying parameters like kernel size, and so on. The non-linear filters, like histogram equalization, can further tune images which are difficult to do with linear filters. Image gradients, introduced in this chapter, are quite common in complex tasks of object detection, image segmentation, and so on. We also saw various transformation methods like translation, rotation and affine transformation with visualization of the output given different choice of parameters. The various transformations can applied in cascaded fashion to create combined transformed results. Lastly, image downsampling and upsampling method is introduced which has crucial role in making computation faster or extracting more richer information respectively.

In the next chapter, we will be going through different features and feature extraction methods with the importance for each.

4
What is a Feature?

In the previous chapter, our main focus was filtering an image and applying different transformations on it. These are good techniques to analyze images but are not sufficient for the majority of computer vision tasks. For example, if we were to make a product detector for a shopping store, computing only edges may not be enough to say whether the image is of an orange or an apple. On the other hand, if a person is given the same task, it is very intuitive to differentiate between an orange and an apple. This is because of the fact that human perception combines several features, such as texture, color, surface, shape, reflections, and so on, to distinguish between one object with another. This motivates to look for more details that relates to complex features of objects. These complex features can then be used in high level image vision tasks like image recognition, search, and so on. There are, however, cases where someone just walks straight into a glass wall, which is due not being able to find enough features to say whether it is free space or glass.

In this chapter, we will first begin with an explanation features and its importance in computer vision. Later in the chapter, we will different types of features extractors like Harris Corner Detector, FAST keypoint detectors, ORB features detectors. The visualization of the keypoints using each of them are also described using OpenCV. Lastly, the effectiveness of ORB features is shown with two similar applications. We will also see a brief discussion on black box features.

Features use cases

Following are some of the generic applications that are popular in computer vision:

- We have two images and we would like to quantify whether these images match each other. Assuming a comparison metric, we say that the image matches when our comparison metric value is greater than a threshold.

- In another example, we have a large database of images, and for a new image, we want to perform an operation similar to matching. Instead of recomputing everything for every image, we can store a smaller, easier to search and robust enough to match, representation of images. This is often referred to as a feature vector of the image. Once a new image comes, we extract similar representation for the new image and search for the nearest match among the previously generated database. This representation is usually formulated in terms of features.

- Also, in the case of finding an object, we have a small image of an object or a region called a **template**. The goal is to check whether an image has this template. This would require matching key points from the template against the given sample image. If the match value is greater than a threshold, we can say the sample image has a region similar to the given template. To further enhance our finding, we can also show where in the sample image lies our template image.

Similarly, a computer vision system needs to learn several features that describes an object such that it is quite easy to distinguish from other objects.

When we design software to do image matching or object detection in images, the basic pipeline for detection is formulated from a machine learning perspective. This means that we take a set of images, extract significant information, learn our model and use the learned model on new images to detect similar objects. In this section, we will explore more on this.

In general, an image matching procedure looks as follows:

- The first step is to extract robust features from a given image. This involves searching through the whole image for possible features and then thresholding them. There are several techniques for the selection of features such as SIFT[3], SURF[4], FAST[5], BRIEF[6], ORB detectors[2], and so on. The feature extracted, in some cases, needs to be converted into a more descriptive form such that it is learnt by the model or can be stored for re-reading.

- In the case of feature matching, we are given a sample image and we would like to see whether this matches a reference image. After feature detection and extraction, as shown previously, a distance metric is formed to compute the distance between features of a sample with respect to the features of reference. If this distance is less than the threshold, we can say the two images are similar.
- For feature tracking, we omit previously explained feature matching steps. Instead of globally matching features, the focus is more on neighborhood matching. This is used in cases such as image stabilization, object tracking, or motion detection.

Datasets and libraries

In this chapter, we will use `OpenCV` library for performing feature detection and matching. The plots are generated using `matplotlib`. We will be using custom images to show the results of various algorithms. However, the code provided here should work on webcam or other custom images too.

Why are features important?

Features play a major role in creating good quality computer vision systems. One of the first features we can think of is **pixels**. In order to create a comparison tool, we use an average of squared distance between the pixel values of two images. These, however, are not robust because rarely will you see two images that are exactly the same. There is always some camera movement and illumination changes between images, and computing a difference between pixel values will be giving out large values even when the images are quite similar.

There are, however, other kinds of features that take into account local and global properties of an image. The local properties are referred to as image statistics around the neighborhood of the image, while global refers to considering overall image statistics. Since both local, and global properties of an image provide significant information about an image, computing features that can capture these will make them more robust and accurate in applications.

The most basic form of feature detector is point features. In applications such as panorama creation on our smartphones, each image is stitched with the corresponding previous image. This stitching of image requires correct orientation of an image overlapped at pixel level accuracy. Computing corresponding pixels between two images requires pixel matching.

Harris Corner Detection

We start feature point detection using the Harris Corner Detection[1] technique. In this, we begin with choosing a matrix, termed a **window**, which is small in size as compared to the image size.

The basic idea is to first overlay chosen window on the input image and observe only the overlayed region from the input image. This window is later shifted over the image and the new overlayed region is observed. In this process, there arise three different cases:

- If there is a flat surface, then we won't be able to see any change in the window region irrespective of the direction of movement of the window. This is because there is no edge or corner in the window region.
- In our second case, the window is overlayed on edge in the image and shifted. If the window moves along the direction of the edge, we will not be able to see any changes in the window. While, if the window is moved in any other direction, we can easily observe changes in the window region.
- Lastly, if the window is overlayed on a corner in the image and is shifted, where the corner is an intersection of two edges, in most of the cases, we will be able to observe the changes in the window region.

Harris Corner Detection uses this property in terms of a score function. Mathematically, it is given as:

$$E[u, v] = \sum_{x,y} w(x, y)[I(x + u)(y + v) + I(x, y)]$$

Where w is a window, u and v are the shift and I is image pixel value. The output E is the objective function and maximizing this with respect to u and v results in corner pixels in the image I.

The Harris Corner Detection score value will show whether there is an edge, corner, or flat surface. An example of Harris Corners of different kinds of images is shown in the following figure:

Harris Corner Visualization

In the previous figure, the upper row has input images, while the bottom row has detected corners. These corners are shown with small gray pixels values corresponding to the location in the input image. In order to generate an image of corners for a given colored image, use the following code:

```
# load image and convert to grayscale
img = cv2.imread('../figures/flower.png')
gray = cv2.cvtColor(img, cv2.COLOR_BGR2GRAY)

# harris corner parameters
block_size = 4 # Covariance matrix size
kernel_size = 3 # neighbourhood kernel
k = 0.01 # parameter for harris corner score

# compute harris corner
corners = cv2.cornerHarris(gray, block_size, kernel_size, k)

# create corner image
display_corner = np.ones(gray.shape[:2])
display_corner = 255*display_corner
# apply thresholding to the corner score
thres = 0.01 # more than 1% of max value
display_corner[corners>thres*corners.max()] = 10 #display pixel value
```

```
# set up display
plt.figure(figsize=(12,8))
plt.imshow(display_corner, cmap='gray')
plt.axis('off')
```

We can generate different number of corners for an image by changing the parameters such as covariance matrix block size, neighbourhood kernel size and Harris score parameter. In the next section, we will see more robust feature detectors.

FAST features

Many features detectors are not useful for real-time applications such as a robot with a camera is moving on the streets. Any delay caused may decrease the functionality of the robot or complete system failure. Features detection is not the only part of the robot system but if this effects the runtime, it can cause significant overhead on other tasks to make it work real time.

FAST (Features from Accelerated Segment Test)[5], was introduced by Edward Rosten and Tom Drummond in 2006. The algorithm uses pixel neighborhood to compute key points in an image. The algorithm for FAST feature detection is as follows:

1. An interesting point candidate pixel **(i,j)** is selected with an intensity $I(i,j)$:

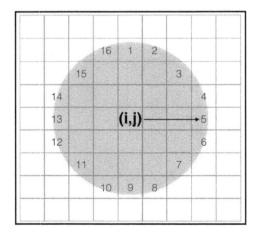

2. In a circle of 16 pixels, given a threshold *t*, estimate *n* adjoining points which are brighter than pixel *(i,j)* intensity by a threshold *t* or darker than *(i,j)* pixel intensity by a threshold *t*. This will become *n* pixels which are either less than *(I(i,j) + t)* or greater than *(I(i,j) - t)*. This *n* was chosen as 12.

3. In a high-speed test, only four pixels (as shown in the figure) at 1, 9, 5, and 13 are looked at. The intensity value of at least three pixels of these decides whether the center pixel *p* is a corner. If these values are either greater than the *(I(i,j) + t)* or less than *(I(i,j) - t)* then the center pixel is considered a corner.

In OpenCV , the steps to compute FAST features are as follows:

1. Initialize detector using `cv2.FastFeatureDetector_create()`
2. Setup threshold parameters for filtering detections
3. Setup flag if non-maximal suppression to be used for clearing neighbourhood regions of repeated detections
4. Detect keypoints and plot them on the input image

In the following figure, there are plots of FAST corners (in small circles) on the input image with varying threshold values. Depending on the image, a different choice of thresholds produce different number of key feature points:

To generate each image in the previous figure, use the following code by changing the threshold values:

```
def compute_fast_det(filename, is_nms=True, thresh = 10):
    """
    Reads image from filename and computes FAST keypoints.
    Returns image with keypoints
    filename: input filename
    is_nms: flag to use Non-maximal suppression
    thresh: Thresholding value
    """
    img = cv2.imread(filename)
    # Initiate FAST object with default values
```

```
fast = cv2.FastFeatureDetector_create()

# find and draw the keypoints
if not is_nms:
    fast.setNonmaxSuppression(0)

fast.setThreshold(thresh)

kp = fast.detect(img,None)
cv2.drawKeypoints(img, kp, img, color=(255,0,0))
return img
```

The following figure shows variations of the same detector across different images with varying thresholds:

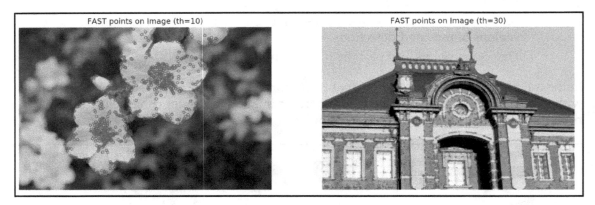

This shows that choice of parameters is quite crucial for different images. Though a common threshold value may not work for all image, a good approximation can be used depending on the similarity of images.

ORB features

Using previously described corner detectors are fast to compute, however in matching two images, it is difficult to select which two image corners are matched for corresponding pixels. An additional information that describes properties a corner is required. A combination of detected keypoints, such as corners, and corresponding descriptors makes comparing images more efficient and robust.

ORB features detection[2] features were described by Ethan Rublee et al. in 2011 and have since been one of the popular features in various applications. This combines two algorithms: FAST feature detector with an orientation component and BRIEF Descriptors, hence the name **Oriented FAST and Rotated BRIEF (ORB)**. The major advantage of using ORB features is the speed of detections while maintaining robust detections. This makes them useful for several real-time applications like robotics vision system, smartphone apps, and so on.

In this chapter we have already seen FAST feature detectors, we will further continue describing BRIEF descriptor and finally build on ORB detector.

FAST feature limitations

FAST Features as described in the previous section computes corner in the image using neighborhood pixels. By creating a comparison test along the circular region around a pixel, features are computed rapidly. FAST features are quite efficient for real-time applications; these do not produce rotation information of the features. This causes a limitation if we are looking for orientation invariant features.

In ORB, FAST features are used with orientation information as well. Using a circular radius of 9 pixels, a vector between computed intensity centroid and center of the corner is used to describe orientation at the given corner. This intensity centroid for a given patch is computed as follows :

- For an image I and a patch window, compute moments using:

$$m_{p,q} = \sum_{x,y} x^p y^q I(x,y)$$

- Using previous moments, intensity centroid of given patch is given as:

$$C = \left(\frac{m_{1,0}}{m_{0,0}} \quad \frac{m_{0,1}}{m_{1,1}} \right)$$

Since, we already know the center O of the patch, a vector joining $\overrightarrow{OC}$ is the orientation of the patch. In further sections, we will see an overall implementation of ORB feature detectors which uses this method.

BRIEF Descriptors and their limitations

The popular feature descriptors like SIFT or SURF outputs large vectors of dimensions 128 and 64 respectively. In applications such as image search, it is quite likely that the features are stored and searched for features rather than the original image. This becomes computationally complex and memory may be inefficient if the number of images reaches a few hundred thousand. In such cases, simple dimensionality reduction is an added step and may reduce overall efficiency. The descriptor proposed by Michael Calonder and their co-authors. in *BRIEF: Binary Robust Independent Elementary Features*[6] resolves issues by consuming less memory.

BRIEF computes differences of intensities in a small patch of an image and represents it as a binary string. This not only makes it faster but also the descriptor preserves good accuracy. However, there is no feature detector in BRIEF but combining it with FAST detectors makes it efficient.

ORB features using OpenCV

The following code uses ORB features implementation in OpenCV.

It is a three-step process, which is described as follows:

- First create an ORB object and update parameter values:

```
orb = cv2.ORB_create()
# set parameters
orb.setScoreType(cv2.FAST_FEATURE_DETECTOR_TYPE_9_16)
```

- Detect keypoints from previously created ORB object:

```
# detect keypoints
kp = orb.detect(img,None)
```

- Lastly, compute descriptors for each keypoints detected:

```
# for detected keypoints compute descriptors.
kp, des = orb.compute(img, kp)
```

The overall code for ORB keypoints detections and descriptor extractor is given as:

```
import numpy as np
import matplotlib.pyplot as plt
import cv2
# With jupyter notebook uncomment below line
```

```
# %matplotlib inline
# This plots figures inside the notebook


def compute_orb_keypoints(filename):
    """
    Reads image from filename and computes ORB keypoints
    Returns image, keypoints and descriptors.
    """
    # load image
    img = cv2.imread(filename)
    # create orb object
    orb = cv2.ORB_create()
    # set parameters
    # FAST feature type
    orb.setScoreType(cv2.FAST_FEATURE_DETECTOR_TYPE_9_16)
    # detect keypoints
    kp = orb.detect(img,None)

    # for detected keypoints compute descriptors.
    kp, des = orb.compute(img, kp)
    return img, kp, des
```

An example of generated keypoints is as shown in the following figure (in circles):

As you can see in the following figure, different images produce different feature points for various shapes of objects:

In order to plot previous shown figures with different keypoints, we can use both OpenCV and Matplotlib as:

```
def draw_keyp(img, kp):
    """
    Takes image and keypoints and plots on the same images
    Does not display it.
    """
    cv2.drawKeypoints(img,kp,img, color=(255,0,0), flags=2)
    return img


def plot_img(img, figsize=(12,8)):
    """
    Plots image using matplotlib for the given figsize
    """
    fig = plt.figure(figsize=figsize)
    ax = fig.add_subplot(1,1,1)

    # image need to be converted to RGB format for plotting
    ax.imshow(cv2.cvtColor(img, cv2.COLOR_BGR2RGB))
    plt.axis('off')
    plt.show()
```

```
def main():
    # read an image
    filename = '../figures/flower.png'
    # compute ORB keypoints
    img1,kp1, des1 = compute_orb_keypoints(filename)
    # draw keypoints on image
    img1 = draw_keyp(img1, kp1)
    # plot image with keypoints
    plot_img(img1)

if __name__ == '__main__':
    main()
```

In this section, we saw formulation of ORB features that not only combines robust features, but also provides descriptors for easier comparison to other features. This is a strong formulation of feature detector, however explicitly designing a feature detector for different task will require efficient choice of parameters such as patch size for FAST detector, BRIEF descriptor parameters etc. For a non-expert, setting these parameters may be quite cumbersome task. In following section, we will begin with discussion on black box features and its importance in creating computer vision systems.

The black box feature

The features we discussed previously are highly dependent on an image to image basis. Some of the challenges observed in detecting features are:

- In case of illumination changes, such as nighttime image or daylight images there would be a significant difference in pixel intensity values as well as neighborhood regions
- As object orientation changes, keypoint descriptor changes significantly. In order to match corresponding features, a proper choice of descriptor parameters is required

Due to these challenges, several parameters used here need to be tuned by experts.

In recent years, a lot has been happening with neural networks in the field of computer vision. The popularity of them has risen due to higher accuracy and less hand-tuned parameters. We can call them black box features—though the term black refers only to the way they are designed. In a majority of these model deployments, the parameters are learned through training and require the least supervision of parameters setting. The black box modeling feature detection helps in getting better features by learning over a dataset of images. This dataset consists of possible different variations of images, as a result the learnt detector can extract better features even in wide variation of image types. We will study these feature detectors in the next chapter as CNNs.

Application – find your object in an image

The most common application for using features is given an object, find the best possible match for it in the image. This is often referred to as **template matching,** where the object at hand is a usually small window called a **template** and goal is to compute the best-matched features from this template to a target image. There exist several solutions to this, but for the sake of understanding, we will use ORB features.

Using ORB features, we can do feature matching in a brute force way as follows:

- Compute features in each image (template and target).
- For each feature in a template, compare all the features in the target detected previously. The criterion is set using a matching score.
- If the feature pair passes the criterion, then they are considered a match.
- Draw matches to visualize.

As a pre-requisite, we will follow previously shown codes for extracting features as:

```python
def compute_orb_keypoints(filename):
    """
    Takes in filename to read and computes ORB keypoints
    Returns image, keypoints and descriptors
    """

    img = cv2.imread(filename)
    # create orb object
    orb = cv2.ORB_create()
    # set parameters
    orb.setScoreType(cv2.FAST_FEATURE_DETECTOR_TYPE_9_16)
    # detect keypoints
    kp = orb.detect(img,None)
```

```
# using keypoints, compute descriptor
kp, des = orb.compute(img, kp)
return img, kp, des
```

Once we have keypoints and descriptors from each of the images, we can use them to compare and match.

Matching keypoints between two images is a two-step process:

- Create desired kind of matcher specifying the distance metric to be used. Here we will use Brute-Force Matching with Hamming distance:

```
bf = cv2.BFMatcher(cv2.NORM_HAMMING2, crossCheck=True)
```

- Using descriptors for keypoints from each image, perform matching as:

```
matches = bf.match(des1,des2)
```

In the following code, we will show overall Brute-Force method of matching keypoints from one image to another using corresponding descriptors only:

```
def brute_force_matcher(des1, des2):
    """
    Brute force matcher to match ORB feature descriptors
    des1, des2: descriptors computed using ORB method for 2 images
    returns matches
    """
    # create BFMatcher object
    bf = cv2.BFMatcher(cv2.NORM_HAMMING2, crossCheck=True)
    # Match descriptors.
    matches = bf.match(des1,des2)

    # Sort them in the order of their distance.
    matches = sorted(matches, key = lambda x:x.distance)

    return matches
```

In the following figure, the features from the template are matched to the original image. To show the effectiveness of matching, only the best matches are shown:

The previous feature matching image is created using the following code, where we use a sample template image to match to a large image of the same object:

```
def compute_img_matches(filename1, filename2, thres=10):
    """
    Extracts ORB features from given filenames
    Computes ORB matches and plot them side by side
    """
    img1, kp1, des1 = compute_orb_keypoints(filename1)
    img2, kp2, des2 = compute_orb_keypoints(filename2)
    matches = brute_force_matcher(des1, des2)
    draw_matches(img1, img2, kp1, kp2, matches, thres)

def draw_matches(img1, img2, kp1, kp2, matches, thres=10):
    """
    Utility function to draw lines connecting matches between two images.
    """
    draw_params = dict(matchColor = (0,255,0),
                       singlePointColor = (255,0,0),
                       flags = 0)

    # Draw first thres matches.
```

```
    img3 = cv2.drawMatches(img1,kp1,img2,kp2,matches[:thres],None,
**draw_params)
    plot_img(img3)


def main():
    # read an image
    filename1 = '../figures/building_crop.jpg'
    filename2 = '../figures/building.jpg'

    compute_img_matches(filename1, filename2)


if __name__ == '__main__':
    main()
```

Applications – is it similar?

In this application, we would like to see if they are similar using previously described feature detectors. For that, we use a similar approach as previously mentioned. The first step is computing feature keypoints and descriptors for each image. Using these performs matching between one image and another. If there are a sufficient number of matches, we can comfortably say that the two images are similar.

For the prerequisites, we use the same ORB keypoint and descriptor extractor but added downsampling of the image:

```
def compute_orb_keypoints(filename):
    """
    Takes in filename to read and computes ORB keypoints
    Returns image, keypoints and descriptors
    """

    img = cv2.imread(filename)
    # downsample image 4x
    img = cv2.pyrDown(img) # downsample 2x
    img = cv2.pyrDown(img) # downsample 4x
    # create orb object
    orb = cv2.ORB_create()
    # set parameters
    orb.setScoreType(cv2.FAST_FEATURE_DETECTOR_TYPE_9_16)
    # detect keypoints
    kp = orb.detect(img,None)
```

```
kp, des = orb.compute(img, kp)
return img, kp,  des
```

Using the previously computed keypoints and descriptors, the matching is done as:

```
def compute_img_matches(filename1, filename2, thres=10):
    """
    Extracts ORB features from given filenames
    Computes ORB matches and plot them side by side
    """
    img1, kp1, des1 = compute_orb_keypoints(filename1)
    img2, kp2, des2 = compute_orb_keypoints(filename2)
    matches = brute_force_matcher(des1, des2)
    draw_matches(img1, img2, kp1, kp2, matches, thres)
def brute_force_matcher(des1, des2):
    """
    Brute force matcher to match ORB feature descriptors
    """
    # create BFMatcher object
    bf = cv2.BFMatcher(cv2.NORM_HAMMING2, crossCheck=True)
    # Match descriptors.
    matches = bf.match(des1,des2)

    # Sort them in the order of their distance.
    matches = sorted(matches, key = lambda x:x.distance)

    return matches

def draw_matches(img1, img2, kp1, kp2, matches, thres=10):
    """
    Utility function to draw lines connecting matches between two images.
    """
    draw_params = dict(matchColor = (0,255,0),
                       singlePointColor = (255,0,0),
                       flags = 0)

    # Draw first thres matches.
    img3 = cv2.drawMatches(img1,kp1,img2,kp2,matches[:thres],None,
**draw_params)
    plot_img(img3)


def main():
    # read an image
    filename2 = '../figures/building_7.JPG'
    filename1 = '../figures/building_crop.jpg'
    compute_img_matches(filename1, filename2, thres=20)
```

```
if __name__ == '__main__':
    main()
```

The results of an example are as shown in the following figure, where inputs are same objects with different viewpoints. The correct matches are shown as with connecting lines:

In this section, we saw two similar approaches for image matching using ORB keypoints and a Brute-Force matcher. The matching can be further enhanced by using more faster algorithms like approximate neighborhood matches. The effect of faster matching is mostly seen in the cases where a large number of features keypoints are extracted.

Summary

In this chapter, we began discussion features and its importance in computer vision applications. Harris Corner Detector is used to detect corners where runtime is of utmost importance. These can run on embedded devices with high speeds. Extending over to more complex detectors, we saw FAST features and in combination with BRIEF descriptors, ORB features can be formed. These are robust for different scales as well as rotations. Finally, we saw the application of feature matching using ORB features and a use of pyramid downsampling.

The discussion on black box features will continue in the next chapter with the introduction of neural networks and especially CNNs.

References

- Harris Chris, and Mike Stephens. *A combined corner and edge detector*. In Alvey vision conference, vol. 15, no. 50, pp. 10-5244. 1988.
- Rublee Ethan, Vincent Rabaud, Kurt Konolige, and Gary Bradski. *ORB: An efficient alternative to SIFT or SURF*. In Computer Vision (ICCV), 2011 IEEE international conference on, pp. 2564-2571. IEEE, 2011.
- Lowe David G. *Object recognition from local scale-invariant features*. In Computer vision, 1999. The proceedings of the seventh IEEE international conference on, vol. 2, pp. 1150-1157. IEEE, 1999.
- Bay Herbert, Tinne Tuytelaars, and Luc Van Gool. *Surf: Speeded up robust features*. Computer vision–ECCV 2006(2006): 404-417.
- Rosten Edward, and Tom Drummond. *Machine learning for high-speed corner detection*. Computer Vision–ECCV 2006(2006): 430-443.
- Calonder Michael, Vincent Lepetit, Christoph Strecha, and Pascal Fua. *Brief: Binary robust independent elementary features*. Computer Vision–ECCV 2010 (2010): 778-792.

5
Convolutional Neural Networks

In the previous chapter, we discussed the importance and applications of features. We now understand that the better the features are, the more accurate the results are going to be. In recent periods, the features have become more precise and as such better accuracy has been achieved. This is due to a new kind of feature extractor called **Convolutional Neural Networks (CNNs)** and they have shown remarkable accuracy in complex tasks, such as object detection in challenging domains, and classifying images with high accuracy, and are now quite ubiquitous in applications ranging from smartphone photo enhancements to satellite image analysis.

In this chapter, we will begin with an introduction to neural nets and continue into an explanation of CNNs and how to implement them. After this chapter, you will be able to write your own CNN from scratch for applications like image classification. The chapter includes:

- Datasets and libraries used in the various sections of the chapter
- Introduction to neural networks with an explanation on simple neural network
- CNN explanation and various components involved in it
- An example of creating CNN for image classification
- Description of transfer learning and statistics on various deep learning models

Datasets and libraries used

In this chapter, we will be using Keras to write neural nets with TensorFlow as backend. A detailed installation procedure is explained in Chapter 2, *Libraries, Development Platforms and Datasets*. To check if you have Keras installed, in shell run:

```
python -c "import keras;print(keras.__version__)"
```

This will print the Keras version as well as which backend you are using. If you have TensorFlow installed and Keras is using TensorFlow, it will print using Tensorflow backend. If you have an older version of Keras and TensorFlow, there might be some issues, so please install or upgrade to the latest versions. We will also be using other libraries like NumPy and OpenCV.

 We will be using the Fashion-MNIST dataset by Zalando SE which is available at https://github.com/zalandoresearch/fashion-mnist. This can be downloaded directly with Keras and there is no requirement for a separate download. Fashion-MNIST is MIT License (MIT) Copyright © [2017] Zalando SE.

Introduction to neural networks

Neural networks have been here for quite some time, with initial papers arriving more than a few decades ago. The recent popularity is due to the availability of better software for algorithms and proper hardware to run them. Initially, neural networks were motivated by how humans perceive the world and were modeled according to biological neuron functions. This was continuously modified over the course of time and has since been evolving to get a better performance.

A simple neural network

A simple neural net consists of a node which takes in an input or a list of inputs and performs a transformation. An example is shown in the following figure:

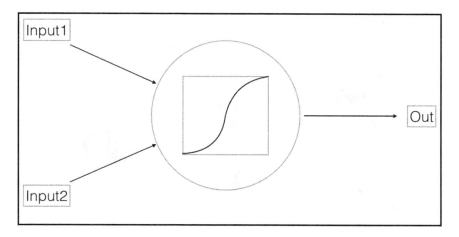

Mathematically, it takes the inputs x and applies a transformation W to get the output y:

$$y = W^T x$$

The input x can be a vector or multi-dimensional array. Based on the transformation matrix W we get the output y to be a vector or multi-dimensional array. This structure is further modified by also including the non-linear transformation F:

$$y = F(W^T x)$$

Now, output y is not linearly dependent on input x, and as a result, the change in x does not proportionally change y. More often, these non-linear transformations consist of clipping all negative values after applying the transformation matrix W to the inputs x. A neuron consists of this complete operation.

These networks are stacked in layered structures, as shown in the following figure:

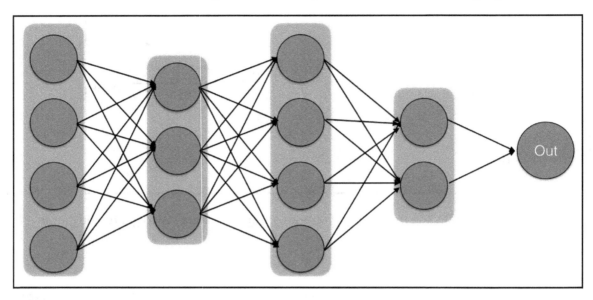

These networks are also termed **feedforward networks**, as there are no loops and input flows through the network in one direction, like in a **Directed Acyclic Graph (DAG)**. In these networks, the parameters are termed as **weights**, which perform a transformation on the inputs.

Using machine learning approaches to learn these weights, we can get an optimal network that performs the desired operation with good accuracy. For this, the requirement is to have a dataset of labeled inputs; for example, for a given input x we already know the output value y. During the learning of the weights of neural networks, also termed as **training**, for this dataset the input is passed through the network layer by layer. At each layer, the input from the previous layer is transformed according to the layer's properties. The final output is our prediction for y and we can measure how far our prediction of y is from the actual value. Once we have this measure, termed as a **loss**, we can then use it to update the weights using a derivative-based approach called **gradient descent**. Each weight is updated according to the change in the loss with respect to weights.

We will describe a simple example of a neural network using `NumPy` library. In this example, we consider the input x a vector of size `1000` and we want to compute an output of size `2`:

```
dim_x = 1000 # input dims
dim_y = 2 # output dims
```

We create a neural network that takes in this input x and applies a non-linear transformation with the weight matrix W:

$$y = \frac{1}{1 + \exp(-W^T x)}$$

An example is shown as follows:

```
def net(x, w):
    """
    A simple neural net that performs non-linear transformation
    Function : 1 / (1 + e^(-w*x))
    x: inputs
    w: weight matrix
    Returns the function value
    """
    return 1/(1+np.exp(-x.dot(w)))
```

To learn these weights `w`, we will follow the gradient descent method. For each input we will compute the gradient of loss with respect to `w` and update the weights as follows:

```
# feed forward pass
y_pred = net(x, w)

# compute loss
loss = compute_loss(y, y_pred)
print("Loss:", loss, "at step:", i)

# compute grads using backprop on given net
w_grad = backprop(y, y_pred, w, x)

# update weights with some learning rate
w -= lr * w_grad
```

This step is iterated repeatedly over our labeled dataset until our loss does not change significantly or the loss values start following some repetition. The `loss` function is defined as:

```python
def compute_loss(y, y_pred):
    """
    Loss function : sum(y_pred**2 - y**2)
    y: ground truth targets
    y_pred: predicted target values
    """
    return np.mean((y_pred-y)**2)
```

The overall code is as follows:

```python
import numpy as np

dim_x = 1000 # input dims
dim_y = 2 # output dims
batch = 10 # batch size for training
lr = 1e-4 # learning rate for weight update
steps = 5000 # steps for learning

# create random input and targets
x = np.random.randn(batch, dim_x)
y = np.random.randn(batch, dim_y)

# initialize weight matrix
w = np.random.randn(dim_x, dim_y)

def net(x, w):
    """
    A simple neural net that performs non-linear transformation
    Function : 1 / (1 + e^(-w*x))
    x: inputs
    w: weight matrix
    Returns the function value
    """
    return 1/(1+np.exp(-x.dot(w)))

def compute_loss(y, y_pred):
    """
    Loss function : sum(y_pred**2 - y**2)
    y: ground truth targets
    y_pred: predicted target values
    """
    return np.mean((y_pred-y)**2)
```

```python
def backprop(y, y_pred, w, x):
    """
    Backpropagation to compute gradients of weights
    y : ground truth targets
    y_pred : predicted targets
    w : weights for the network
    x : inputs to the net
    """
    # start from outer most
    y_grad = 2.0 * (y_pred - y)

    # inner layer grads
    w_grad = x.T.dot(y_grad * y_pred * (1 - y_pred))
    return w_grad

for i in range(steps):

    # feed forward pass
    y_pred = net(x, w)

    # compute loss
    loss = compute_loss(y, y_pred)
    print("Loss:", loss, "at step:", i)

    # compute grads using backprop on given net
    w_grad = backprop(y, y_pred, w, x)

    # update weights with some learning rate
    w -= lr * w_grad
```

On running the previous code, we can see the values of loss decreasing and settling down. The parameters here are learning rate and initial w values. A good choice for these values may cause the loss to decrease faster and settle early; however, a bad choice will lead to no decrease in loss, or sometimes an increase in loss over several iterations.

In this section, we have seen how to build a simple neural network. You can use this code and modify or add complex structures to play with it. Before we go further, to the explanation for CNNs, in the next section we will briefly revisit the convolution operation, which was explained in the previous chapter.

Revisiting the convolution operation

Extending our discussion on filters from Chapter 3, *Image Filtering and Transformations in OpenCV*, the convolution operation is taking a dot product of a shifted kernel matrix with a given input image. This process is explained in the following figure:

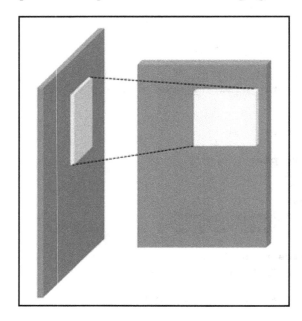

As shown in the previous figure, a kernel is a small two-dimensional array that computes dot product with the input image (on the left) to create a block of the output image (on the right).

In convolution, the output image is generated by taking a dot product between an **Input** image and a **Kernel** matrix. This is then shifted along the image and after each shift, corresponding values of the output are generated using a dot product:

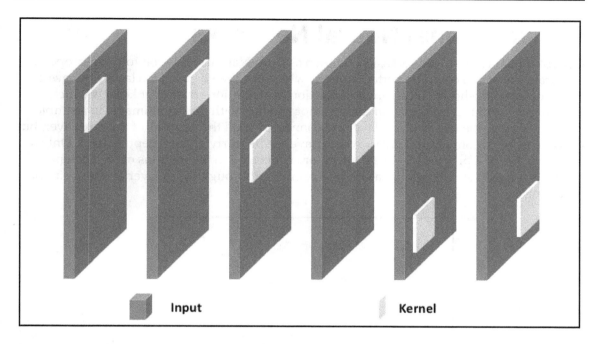

As we saw in the previous chapter, we can perform a convolution operation using OpenCV as follows:

```
kernel = np.ones((5,5),np.float32)/25
dst = cv2.filter2D(gray,-1,kernel)
```

Here, we assume a kernel with equal values whose sum is 1 and is used to perform convolution on a grayscale image. In Chapter 3, *Image Filtering and Transformations in OpenCV*, this was termed as **smoothing operation** because if we have a noisy grayscale image, the output will look smoother.

In this case, to perform a smoothing operation we already know the kernel values. If we know the kernels for extracting more complex features, we can do better inference from images. However, manually setting the values is unfeasible when we have to perform tasks like image classification and object detection. In such cases, models such as CNNs extract good features and perform better than other previous methods. In the next section, we will define a structure that will learn these kernel matrix values and compute richer features for a wide variety of applications.

Convolutional Neural Networks

Convolutional Neural Networks, also known as **ConvNets**, use this convolution property in a neural network to compute better features, which can then be used to classify images or detect objects. As shown in the previous section, convolution consists of kernels which compute an output by sliding and taking a dot product with the input image. In a simple neural network, the neurons of a layer are connected to all the neurons of the next layer, but CNNs consist of convolution layers which have the property of the receptive field. Only a small portion of a previous layer's neurons are connected to the neurons of the current layer. As a result, small region features are computed through every layer as shown in the following figure:

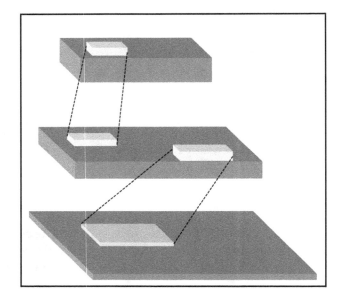

As we have seen in a simple neural network, the neuron takes an input from one or more of previous neurons' output to perform a non-linear transformation. In CNNs, this is further combined with the convolution approach. We assume a set of kernels with varied values called **weights**. Each of these kernels is convolved with an input to create a response matrix. There is then a non-linear transformation called **activation** for each of the values in the convolved output. The output from each of the kernels after activation is stacked to create the output of our operation such that for K kernels the output is of $K \ x \ H_o \ x \ W_o$ size, with H_o and W_o as the height and width of our output. This makes one layer of CNN.

The output from the previous layer is then used again as the input for the next layer with another set of kernels K_2, and a new response is computed by first convolving each of the kernels and then taking the non-linear transformation of the response.

In general, CNNs are composed of the following types of layers:

- Convolutional layers
- Fully connected layers
- Activation layers
- Pooling layers

Each of these layers will be explained in the following sections. In recent developments, some more components have been added to CNNs, but the preceding components still remain important.

The convolution layer

A key component of a CNN is the convolution layer, which performs a dot product of a kernel matrix with part of an image and generates an output. This is followed by shifting and repeating the same operation over a complete image and is termed **convolution**. The region of the input which is taken for the dot product is called the **receptive field** of the convolution layer. In each convolution layer, there is a set of kernels and they are collectively termed **filters**.

The input for a convolution layer is an n-dimensional array, meaning the input is an image of the form *Width x Height x Depth*. For example, if we have a grayscale image of the size 32 x 32, width and height, then the input is 32 x 32 x 1 where depth is the number of color channels in this case, and is represented by the third dimension. Similarly, for a colored image of size 512, the input is 512 x 512 x 3. All the kernels in filters also have the same depth as the input.

The parameters for the layer are the number of filters, filter size, strides, and padding value. Of these, *filter* values are the only learnable parameters. *Strides* refer to the amount of shift in pixels for a kernel. With a stride of 1, the kernel is moved left by 1 pixel and the dot product is taken with the corresponding input region. With a stride of 2, the kernel is moved by 2 pixels and the same operation takes place. On each input, at the boundary, the kernel can only overlap a certain region inside the image. Boundaries are therefore padded with zeros for the kernel to capture the complete image region. The padding value sets the way to pad the image boundary.

The size of the output depends on these parameter values. We can use Keras to write CNN and perform operations on images. An example of writing one convolution layer is:

```
y = Conv2D(filters=32,
           kernel_size=(5,5),
           strides=1, padding="same")(x)
```

Let's create an example model to see the properties of convolution layer:

```
from keras.layers import Conv2D, Input
from keras.models import Model

def print_model():
    """
    Creates a sample model and prints output shape
    Use this to analyse convolution parameters
    """
    # create input with given shape
    x = Input(shape=(512,512,3))

    # create a convolution layer
    y = Conv2D(filters=32,
               kernel_size=(5,5),
               strides=1, padding="same",
               use_bias=False)(x)
    # create model
    model = Model(inputs=x, outputs=y)

    # prints our model created
    model.summary()

print_model()
```

When you execute codes, please ignore the warnings shown, such as: Your CPU supports instructions that this TensorFlow binary was not compiled to use: SSE4.1 SSE4.2 AVX AVX2 FMA.

On executing this code, we can see our model and output after each layer as:

```
Layer (type) Output Shape Param #
===================================================================
input_1 (InputLayer) (None, 512, 512, 3) 0

conv2d_1 (Conv2D) (None, 512, 512, 32) 2400
===================================================================
Total params: 2,400
Trainable params: 2,400
Non-trainable params: 0
```

Here, we have set the input to be of the shape 512 x 512 x 3, and for convolution, we use 32 filters with the size 5 x 5. The stride values we have set to 1, and using the same padding for the edges, we make sure a kernel captures all of the images. We will not use bias for this example. The output after convolution is of the shape (None, 512, 512, 32) of the shape (samples, width, height, filters). For the discussion, we will ignore the sample's value. The width and height of the output is 512 with the depth as 32. The number of filters we used to set the output's depth value. The total number of parameters for this layer is 5 x 5 x 3 x 32 (kernel_size * number of filters) which is 2400.

Let's try another run. Now, we set strides to 2 in the previous code. On execution, we get the output as:

```
Layer (type) Output Shape Param #
===================================================================
input_1 (InputLayer) (None, 512, 512, 3) 0

conv2d_1 (Conv2D) (None, 256, 256, 32) 2400
===================================================================
Total params: 2,400
Trainable params: 2,400
Non-trainable params: 0
```

As we can see, the convolution output shape (width, height) is reduced to half of the input size. This is due to the stride option that we have chosen. Using strides 2, it will skip one pixel, making the output half of the input. Let's increase the stride to 4. The output will be:

```
Layer (type) Output Shape Param #
=================================================================
input_1 (InputLayer) (None, 512, 512, 3) 0

conv2d_1 (Conv2D) (None, 128, 128, 32) 2400
=================================================================
Total params: 2,400
Trainable params: 2,400
Non-trainable params: 0
```

Here, we can see that the output shape (width and height) is reduced to one-fourth of the input.

If we set our strides to 1, and padding to valid, the output is:

```
Layer (type) Output Shape Param #
=================================================================
input_1 (InputLayer) (None, 512, 512, 3) 0

conv2d_1 (Conv2D) (None, 508, 508, 32) 2400
=================================================================
Total params: 2,400
Trainable params: 2,400
Non-trainable params: 0
```

Now, even if we set strides to 1, the output shape (width and height) is reduced to 508. This is due to the lack of a padding set, and the kernel cannot be applied to the edges of the input.

We can compute the output shape as $(I - K + 2P)/S + 1$, where I is input size, K is kernel size, P is padding used and S is stride value. If we use the same padding, the P value is $(K - 1)/2$. Otherwise, if we use the valid padding then P value is zero.

Here, we have set another parameter `use_bias=False`. On setting this as true, it will add a constant value to each kernel and for a convolution layer, the bias parameter is the same as the number of filters used. So, if we set `use_bias to True`, with strides 1 and the same padding, we get:

```
Layer (type) Output Shape Param #
=================================================================
input_1 (InputLayer) (None, 512, 512, 3) 0
_____
conv2d_1 (Conv2D) (None, 512, 512, 32) 2432
=================================================================
Total params: 2,432
Trainable params: 2,432
Non-trainable params: 0
```

The total number of parameters is increased by 32, which is the number of filters used in this layer. We have seen how to design the convolution layer and what happens when we use different parameters for the convolution layer.

The crucial thing is, what are the kernel values in the filters that will give the desired output? To have good performance, we would like to get the output to consist of high-quality features from the input. Setting values for the filters manually is not feasible as the number of filters grows quite large and the combinations of these values are practically infinite. We learn the filter values using optimization techniques which use a dataset of inputs and targets and tries to predict as close to the targets as possible. The optimization then updates the weights after each iteration.

The activation layer

As we saw in the case of the simple neural network, the weighted output is passed through a non-linear transformation. This non-linear layer is often referred to as the activation layer. Some common types of activation are:

- Sigmoid: $f(x) = 1/(1 + e^{-x})$
- ReLU: $f(x) = \max(0, x)$

- Tanh: $f(x) = \tanh(x)$
- Leaky ReLU: $f(x) = \max(\alpha x, x)$ where α is a small positive float
- Softmax: $f(x)_i = e^{x_i} / \sum_i e^{x_i}$ this is often used to represent probability for a class

The most common choice of activation function is **Rectified Linear Unit (ReLU)** and this performs well in the majority of cases. In our previous code we can add an activation layer as follows:

```python
from keras.layers import Conv2D, Input, Activation
from keras.models import Model

def print_model():
    """
    Creates a sample model and prints output shape
    Use this to analyse convolution parameters
    """
    # create input with given shape
    x = Input(shape=(512,512,3))

    # create a convolution layer
    conv = Conv2D(filters=32,
                  kernel_size=(5,5),
                  strides=1, padding="same",
                  use_bias=True)(x)
    # add activation layer
    y = Activation('relu')(conv)
    # create model
    model = Model(inputs=x, outputs=y)

    # prints our model created
    model.summary()

print_model()
```

The output of executing the code is as follows:

```
Layer (type) Output Shape Param #
================================================================
input_1 (InputLayer) (None, 512, 512, 3) 0

conv2d_1 (Conv2D) (None, 512, 512, 32) 2432

activation_1 (Activation) (None, 512, 512, 32) 0
================================================================
Total params: 2,432
Trainable params: 2,432
Non-trainable params: 0
```

As we can see from our formulation of activation functions, it does not contain any trainable parameters. In Keras, the activation layer can also be added to the convolution layer as follows:

```
conv = Conv2D(filters=32,
              kernel_size=(5,5), activation="relu",
              strides=1, padding="same",
              use_bias=True)(x)
```

The pooling layer

Pooling takes in a region of inputs and either a max or an average value of that region is produced as output. In effect, it reduces the size of an input by sampling in the local region. This layer is inserted between 2 to 3 convolution layers to reduce the resolution of the output, thereby reducing the requirement for parameters. A visual representation of the pooling operation is as follows:

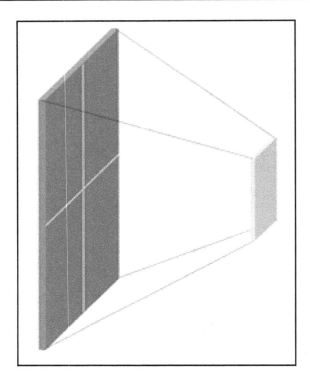

In the previous figure, the input is a two-dimensional array of 2 x 2 size and after pooling operation the output is of size 1 x 1. This can be generated by taking average of the values in the previous array or the maximum value.

To show how the output shape changes after this operation, we can use the following code:

```python
from keras.layers import Conv2D, Input, MaxPooling2D
from keras.models import Model

def print_model():
    """
    Creates a sample model and prints output shape
    Use this to analyse Pooling parameters
    """
    # create input with given shape
    x = Input(shape=(512,512,3))

    # create a convolution layer
    conv = Conv2D(filters=32,
            kernel_size=(5,5), activation="relu",
            strides=1, padding="same",
```

```
                use_bias=True)(x)

    pool = MaxPooling2D(pool_size=(2,2))(conv)
    # create model
    model = Model(inputs=x, outputs=pool)

    # prints our model created
    model.summary()

print_model()
```

In the previous code, we used a convolution layer and added a pooling operation to it. When we execute it, the expected output is:

```
Layer (type) Output Shape Param #
==================================================================
input_1 (InputLayer) (None, 512, 512, 3) 0

conv2d_1 (Conv2D) (None, 512, 512, 32) 2432

max_pooling2d_1 (MaxPooling2 (None, 256, 256, 32) 0
==================================================================
Total params: 2,432
Trainable params: 2,432
Non-trainable params: 0
```

Here, we set the pooling parameter to (2,2), representing the width and height of the pooling operation. The depth for pooling will be set according to the depth of the input to the pooling layer. The resulting output is of half the shape in terms of width and height; however, there is no change in depth size.

The fully connected layer

This is a simple neural network layer where each neuron in the current layer is connected to all the neurons in the previous layer. This is often referred to as `Dense` or `Linear` in various deep learning libraries. In Keras, this can be implemented as follows:

```
from keras.layers import Dense, Input
from keras.models import Model

def print_model():
    """
    Creates a sample model and prints output shape
    Use this to analyse dense/Fully Connected parameters
    """
    # create input with given shape
    x = Input(shape=(512,))

    # create a fully connected layer layer
    y = Dense(32)(x)
    # create model
    model = Model(inputs=x, outputs=y)

    # prints our model created
    model.summary()

print_model()
```

As we execute this code, we can see the output shapes, as well as the number of trainable parameters, as follows:

```
Layer (type) Output Shape Param #
================================================================
input_1 (InputLayer) (None, 512) 0
_____
dense_1 (Dense) (None, 32) 16416
================================================================
Total params: 16,416
Trainable params: 16,416
Non-trainable params: 0
_____
```

The total parameters for this layer are given by $(I_s * O_s) + O_s$ where I_s is input shape and O_s is output shape. In our example, we used an input of shape 512 and an output of shape 32 and get a total of 16416 parameters with bias. This is quite large compared to a similar convolution layer block, therefore in recent models, there has been a trend towards using more convolution blocks rather than fully connected blocks. Nonetheless, this layer still plays a major role in designing simple convolution neural net blocks.

In this section, we saw what CNNs are and what their components are. However, we haven't seen a way to set parameter values. Additionally, we have not seen several other layer structures, such as Batch Normalization and Dropout. These other layers also play major roles in designing CNN models.

Batch Normalization

This is applied to normalize the output from the input layer with mean 0 and variance 1 as:

$$\hat{x}^{(k)} = \frac{x^{(k)} - \mu_k}{\sqrt{\sigma_k^2 + \epsilon}}$$

This layer also has learnable parameters (which are optional in most of the deep learning libraries) to squash output in a given range:

$$y^{(k)} = \gamma^{(k)} \hat{x}^{(k)} + \beta^{(k)}$$

Here γ and β are learnable parameters. Batch Normalization improves training by faster convergence as well as acting as a kind of regularization. However, since there are learnable parameters, the effect of normalization is different in training and testing.

Dropout

One of the important layers that helps prevent overfitting is Dropout. It randomly drops, with some probability, the neurons from the previous layer to be used as input to the next layer. This acts like we are training an ensemble of neural networks.

In the following section, we will see how to implement a model in Keras and perform the learning of parameters, which we skipped in this section.

CNN in practice

We will now start with our implementation of a convolutional neural net in Keras. For our example case, we will train a network to classify `Fashion-MNIST`. This is a dataset of grayscale images of fashion products, of the size 28 x 28. The total number of images is 70,000, with 60,000 as training and 10,000 as a test. There are ten categories in this dataset, which are t-shirt, trousers, pullover, dress, coat, sandal, shirt, sneakers, bag, and ankle boots. Labels for each are marked with a category number from 0-9.

We can load this dataset as follows:

```
from keras.datasets import fashion_mnist
(x_train, y_train), (x_test, y_test) = fashion_mnist.load_data()
```

The previous code block doesn't output a visualization of the dataset, so following image is to show what dataset we will be using:

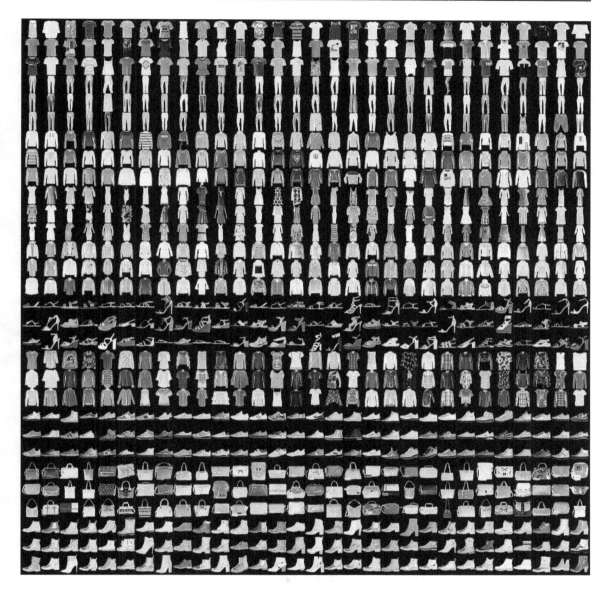

It will split the data into the train and test sets with both inputs x as well as the label y.

The convolution layer is written as follows:

```python
def conv3x3(input_x,nb_filters):
    """
    Wrapper around convolution layer
    Inputs:
        input_x: input layer / tensor
        nb_filter: Number of filters for convolution
    """
    return Conv2D(nb_filters, kernel_size=(3,3), use_bias=False,
            activation='relu', padding="same")(input_x)
```

The pooling layer is written as follows:

```python
x = MaxPooling2D(pool_size=(2,2))(input)
```

The overall output layer is as follows:

```python
preds = Dense(nb_class, activation='softmax')(x)
```

The complete model is as follows:

```python
def create_model(img_h=28, img_w=28):
    """
    Creates a CNN model for training.
    Inputs:
        img_h: input image height
        img_w: input image width
    Returns:
        Model structure
    """
    inputs = Input(shape=(img_h, img_w, 1))

    x = conv3x3(inputs, 32)
    x = conv3x3(x, 32)
    x = MaxPooling2D(pool_size=(2,2))(x)
    x = conv3x3(x, 64)
    x = conv3x3(x, 64)
    x = MaxPooling2D(pool_size=(2,2))(x)
    x = conv3x3(x, 128)
    x = MaxPooling2D(pool_size=(2,2))(x)
    x = Flatten()(x)
    x = Dense(128, activation="relu")(x)
    preds = Dense(nb_class, activation='softmax')(x)
    model = Model(inputs=inputs, outputs=preds)
    print(model.summary())
    return model
```

On running the previous code block, created model can be seen as, where each row is a layer type arranged sequentially with input layer on the top:

```
Layer (type) Output Shape Param #
=================================================================
input_1 (InputLayer) (None, 28, 28, 1) 0
_____
conv2d_1 (Conv2D) (None, 28, 28, 32) 288
_____
conv2d_2 (Conv2D) (None, 28, 28, 32) 9216
_____
max_pooling2d_1 (MaxPooling2 (None, 14, 14, 32) 0
_____
conv2d_3 (Conv2D) (None, 14, 14, 64) 18432
_____
conv2d_4 (Conv2D) (None, 14, 14, 64) 36864
_____
max_pooling2d_2 (MaxPooling2 (None, 7, 7, 64) 0
_____
conv2d_5 (Conv2D) (None, 7, 7, 128) 73728
_____
max_pooling2d_3 (MaxPooling2 (None, 3, 3, 128) 0
_____
flatten_1 (Flatten) (None, 1152) 0
_____
dense_1 (Dense) (None, 128) 147584
_____
dense_2 (Dense) (None, 10) 1290
=================================================================
Total params: 287,402
Trainable params: 287,402
Non-trainable params: 0
```

Fashion-MNIST classifier training code

In the section, we will see a classifier model on `Fashion-MNIST` dataset. This will take in input grayscale image and outputs one of the pre-defined 10 classes. In the following steps, we will build the model:

1. First, we import the relevant libraries and modules:

```
import keras
import keras.backend as K
from keras.layers import Dense, Conv2D, Input, MaxPooling2D,
```

```
Flatten
from keras.models import Model
from keras.datasets import fashion_mnist
from keras.callbacks import ModelCheckpoint
```

2. We define the input height and width parameters to be used throughout, as well as other parameters. Here, an epoch defines one iteration over all of the data. So, the number of epochs means the total number of iterations over all of the data:

```
# setup parameters
batch_sz = 128  # batch size
nb_class = 10  # target number of classes
nb_epochs = 10 # training epochs
img_h, img_w = 28, 28  # input dimensions
```

3. Let's download and prepare the dataset for training and validation. There is already an inbuilt function to do this in Keras:

```
def get_dataset():
    """
    Return processed and reshaped dataset for training
    In this cases Fashion-mnist dataset.
    """
    # load mnist dataset
    (x_train, y_train), (x_test, y_test) =
fashion_mnist.load_data()
    # test and train datasets
    print("Nb Train:", x_train.shape[0], "Nb
test:",x_test.shape[0])
    x_train = x_train.reshape(x_train.shape[0], img_h, img_w, 1)
    x_test = x_test.reshape(x_test.shape[0], img_h, img_w, 1)
    in_shape = (img_h, img_w, 1)

    # normalize inputs
    x_train = x_train.astype('float32')
    x_test = x_test.astype('float32')
    x_train /= 255.0
    x_test /= 255.0

    # convert to one hot vectors
    y_train = keras.utils.to_categorical(y_train, nb_class)
    y_test = keras.utils.to_categorical(y_test, nb_class)
    return x_train, x_test, y_train, y_test

x_train, x_test, y_train, y_test = get_dataset()
```

4. We will build the model using the wrapper convolution function defined earlier:

```
def conv3x3(input_x,nb_filters):
    """
    Wrapper around convolution layer
    Inputs:
        input_x: input layer / tensor
        nb_filter: Number of filters for convolution
    """
    return Conv2D(nb_filters, kernel_size=(3,3), use_bias=False,
            activation='relu', padding="same")(input_x)

def create_model(img_h=28, img_w=28):
    """
    Creates a CNN model for training.
    Inputs:
        img_h: input image height
        img_w: input image width
    Returns:
        Model structure
    """
    inputs = Input(shape=(img_h, img_w, 1))

    x = conv3x3(inputs, 32)
    x = conv3x3(x, 32)
    x = MaxPooling2D(pool_size=(2,2))(x)
    x = conv3x3(x, 64)
    x = conv3x3(x, 64)
    x = MaxPooling2D(pool_size=(2,2))(x)
    x = conv3x3(x, 128)
    x = MaxPooling2D(pool_size=(2,2))(x)
    x = Flatten()(x)
    x = Dense(128, activation="relu")(x)
    preds = Dense(nb_class, activation='softmax')(x)
    model = Model(inputs=inputs, outputs=preds)
    print(model.summary())
    return model

model = create_model()
```

5. Let's set up the optimizer, loss function, and metrics to evaluate our predictions:

```
# setup optimizer, loss function and metrics for model
model.compile(loss=keras.losses.categorical_crossentropy,
            optimizer=keras.optimizers.Adam(),
            metrics=['accuracy'])
```

6. This is optional if we would like to save our model after every epoch:

```
# To save model after each epoch of training
callback = ModelCheckpoint('mnist_cnn.h5')
```

7. Let's begin training our model:

```
# start training
model.fit(x_train, y_train,
          batch_size=batch_sz,
          epochs=nb_epochs,
          verbose=1,
          validation_data=(x_test, y_test),
          callbacks=[callback])
```

8. The previous piece of code will run for a while if you are using the only CPU. After 10 epochs, it will say `val_acc= 0.92` (approximately). This means our trained model can perform with about 92% accuracy on unseen `Fashion-MNIST` data.

9. Once all epoch training finishes, final evaluation is computed as:

```
# Evaluate and print accuracy
score = model.evaluate(x_test, y_test, verbose=0)
print('Test loss:', score[0])
print('Test accuracy:', score[1])
```

Analysis of CNNs

Research on different kinds of CNNs is still ongoing, and year after year we see improvements in accuracy for models on complex datasets. These improvements are in terms of both model structure and how to train these models effectively.

Popular CNN architectures

In the recent few years, the following have become popular in various practical applications. In this section, we will see some of the popular architectures and how to load them in Keras.

VGGNet

This was introduced in 2014 by Karen Simonyan and Andrew Zisserman, in the paper *Very Deep Convolution Networks for Large-Scale Image Recognition,* `https://arxiv.org/abs/1409.1556`.

This was one of the initial papers that improved the performance of object classification models and was one of the top performing models in the **Imagenet Large Scale Visual Recognition Challenge (ILSVRC)** 2014, the dataset for this was introduced in `Chapter 2`, *Libraries, Development Platform, and Datasets*. The performance gain was about 4% from the previous best model, and as a result, it became quite popular. There were several versions of the model but the most popular are VGG16 and VGG19. We can see a pretrained VGG16 model in Keras:

```
from keras.applications.vgg16 import VGG16

def print_model():
    """
    Loads VGGNet and prints model structure
    """
    # create model
    model = VGG16(weights='imagenet')

    # prints our model created
    model.summary()

print_model()
```

On execution, we can see the output as follows:

Layer (type)	Output Shape	Param #
input_1 (InputLayer)	(None, 224, 224, 3)	0
block1_conv1 (Conv2D)	(None, 224, 224, 64)	1792
block1_conv2 (Conv2D)	(None, 224, 224, 64)	36928
block1_pool (MaxPooling2D)	(None, 112, 112, 64)	0
block2_conv1 (Conv2D)	(None, 112, 112, 128)	73856
block2_conv2 (Conv2D)	(None, 112, 112, 128)	147584
block2_pool (MaxPooling2D)	(None, 56, 56, 128)	0

```
block3_conv1 (Conv2D) (None, 56, 56, 256) 295168

block3_conv2 (Conv2D) (None, 56, 56, 256) 590080

block3_conv3 (Conv2D) (None, 56, 56, 256) 590080

block3_pool (MaxPooling2D) (None, 28, 28, 256) 0

block4_conv1 (Conv2D) (None, 28, 28, 512) 1180160

block4_conv2 (Conv2D) (None, 28, 28, 512) 2359808

block4_conv3 (Conv2D) (None, 28, 28, 512) 2359808

block4_pool (MaxPooling2D) (None, 14, 14, 512) 0

block5_conv1 (Conv2D) (None, 14, 14, 512) 2359808

block5_conv2 (Conv2D) (None, 14, 14, 512) 2359808

block5_conv3 (Conv2D) (None, 14, 14, 512) 2359808

block5_pool (MaxPooling2D) (None, 7, 7, 512) 0

flatten (Flatten) (None, 25088) 0

fc1 (Dense) (None, 4096) 102764544

fc2 (Dense) (None, 4096) 16781312

predictions (Dense) (None, 1000) 4097000
=================================================================
Total params: 138,357,544
Trainable params: 138,357,544
Non-trainable params: 0
```

Since the total number of parameters is quite large, training such a model from scratch will also require a huge amount of data of the order of a few hundred thousand.

Inception models

These were successful in using parallel structures in the convolution network, which further increased the performance of models in the same competition. It was proposed and refined by Christian Szegedy, Vincent Vanhoucke, Sergey Ioffe, Jonathon Shlens, Zbigniew Wojna in the paper *Rethinking the Inception Architecture for Computer Vision,* `https://arxiv.org/abs/1512.00567`. The model structure for inception-v3 is as follows:

We can use this model in Keras:

```python
from keras.applications.inception_v3 import InceptionV3

def print_model():
    """
    Loads InceptionV3 model and prints model structure
    """
    # create model
    model = InceptionV3(weights='imagenet')

    # prints our model created
    model.summary()

print_model()
```

On execution, it will print out the model structure.

ResNet model

Extending more on parallel structure, Kaiming He, Xiangyu Zhang, Shaoqing Ren, Jian Sun. introduced *Deep Residual Learning for Image Recognition* `https://arxiv.org/abs/1512.` `03385` that uses skip connection. The basic block of ResNet is as follows:

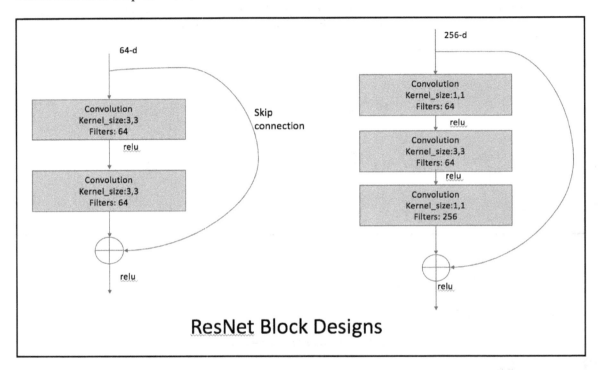

These blocks are repeated and stacked over to create a large network with a depth of 18 for 18 blocks, 50 for 50 blocks, and so on. They have shown remarkable performance both in terms of accuracy and computation time. In the following code, we will see how to use this to predict the top-5 probable categories from an image.

The input to the model is the following image of a train locomotive engine, which is any normal smartphone photo. We want to see if the pretrained ResNet-50 model can do close to ground truth predictions:

Let's load the required imports as:

```
from keras.applications.resnet50 import ResNet50
import numpy as np
import cv2
from keras.applications.resnet50 import preprocess_input,
decode_predictions
import time
```

We now begin creating a model to detect object in previously shown figure:

1. The first thing we do is setup loading the ResNet-50 pretrained model:

```
def get_model():
    """
    Loads Resnet and prints model structure
    Returns resnet as model.
```

```
"""
# create model
model = ResNet50(weights='imagenet')

# To print our model loaded
model.summary()
return model
```

2. We need to preprocess the image for a specific input type for ResNet. In this case, the input is the mean, normalized to the size (1, 224, 224, 3):

```
def preprocess_img(img):
    # apply opencv preprocessing
    img = cv2.cvtColor(img, cv2.COLOR_BGR2RGB)
    img = cv2.resize(img, (224, 224))
    img = img[np.newaxis, :, :, :]
    # convert to float type
    img = np.asarray(img, dtype=np.float)
    # further use imagenet specific preprocessing
    # this applies color channel specific mean normalization
    x = preprocess_input(img)
    print(x.shape)
    return x
```

3. Let's go ahead and load the image and apply preprocessing:

```
# read input image and preprocess
img = cv2.imread('../figures/train1.png')
input_x = preprocess_img(img)
```

4. We will now load the model and pass the processed input through the trained model. This also computes the runtime:

```
# create model with pretrained weights
resnet_model = get_model()

# run predictions only , no training
start = time.time()
preds = resnet_model.predict(input_x)
print(time.time() - start)
```

5. We have got predictions, but these are just probability values and not class names. We will now print class names corresponding to only the top-5 probable predictions:

```
# decode prediction to index of classes, top 5 predictions
print('Predicted:', decode_predictions(preds, top=5)[0])
```

The output for this is as follows:

```
Predicted: [('n04310018', 'steam_locomotive', 0.89800948), ('n03895866',
'passenger_car', 0.066653267), ('n03599486', 'jinrikisha', 0.0083348891),
('n03417042', 'garbage_truck', 0.0052676937), ('n04266014',
'space_shuttle', 0.0040852665)]
```

n04310018 and steam_locomotive are the class index and names. The value denoted after that is the probability for prediction. So, the pretrained model is 89% probable that the input image is a steam locomotive. This is quite impressive since the input image is of a locomotive which is not in service and has probably never been seen by the model during training.

Transfer learning

In the previous section we saw three different model types, but in deep learning models, we are not limited to these. Every year there are better performing model architectures being published. However, the performance of these models totally depends on training data and their performance is due to the millions of images they are trained on. Getting such large datasets and training them for task specific purposes is not cost effective, as well as being time consuming. Nonetheless, the models can be used in various domains by doing a special type of training called **transfer learning**.

In transfer learning, we fix a part of a model from the input to a given layer (also known as **freezing a model**), such that the pretrained weights will help in computing rich features from the image. The remaining part is trained on task specific datasets. As a result, the remaining part of the model learns better features even with small datasets. The choice of how much of a model to freeze depends on available datasets and repeated experimentation.

Further, we will show a comparison of previous models, to understand better which model to use. The first plot is the number of parameters in each of the models. As the newer models were released, they became more efficient in terms of number of parameters to train:

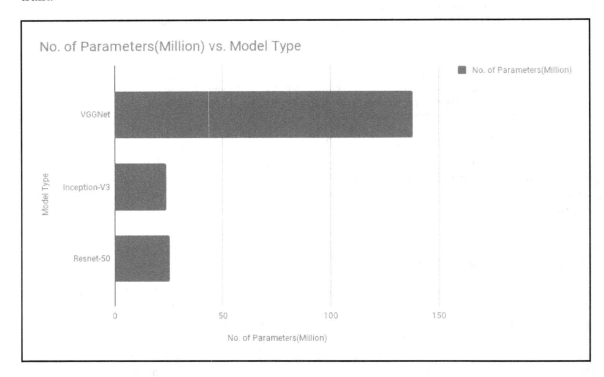

Also, we show the comparison of accuracy for the ILSVRC challenge across different years. This shows that the model gets better with less parameters and better model structures:

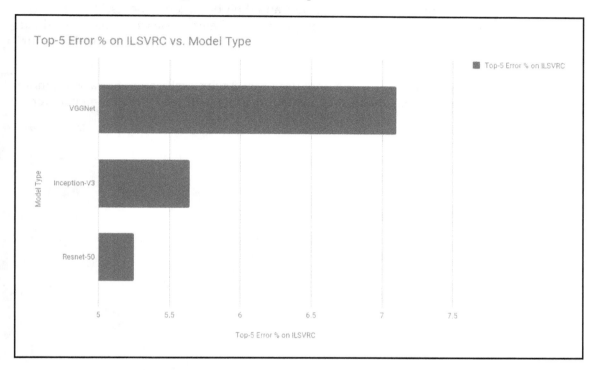

In this section, we saw that even lacking of large dataset for a particular task, we can still achieve good performance by transferring the learning from model trained on other similar dataset. In most practical applications, we use models trained on ImageNet dataset, however choice of model is, decided by the user, based on criteria such as more accuracy model or faster model.

Summary

In this chapter, we had an introduction to CNNs and their basic components. We also saw how to train a model from scratch on an example dataset. Later, we learnt to use pretrained models to perform prediction and also transfer learning to re-utilize trained models for our tasks.

These trained models and CNNs are not only used for image classification but also on more complex tasks like object detection and segmentation, as we will see in upcoming chapters.

6
Feature-Based Object Detection

In the previous chapter, we understood the importance of and how to model deep layered feature extraction using **Convolutional Neural Networks** (**CNNs**). In this chapter, we will learn how to model a CNN to detect where the object in the image is and also classify the object in one of our pre-decided categories.

In this chapter:

- We will begin with a general discussion on image recognition and what is object detection
- A working example of the popular techniques for face detection using OpenCV
- Object detection using two-stage models such as Faster-RCNN
- Object detection using one-stage model such as SSD
- The major part of this chapter will be discussing deep learning-based object detectors and explaining them using a code for the demo

Introduction to object detection

To begin with object detection, we will first see an overview of image recognition as detection is one part of it. In the following figure, an overview of object recognition is described using an image from `Pascal VOC` dataset. The input is passes through a model which then produces information in four different styles:

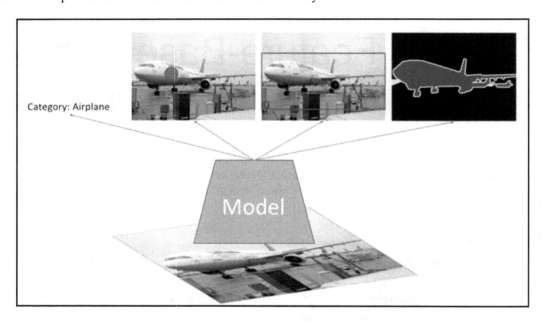

The model in the previous image performs generic image recognition where we can predict the following information:

- A class name for the object in the image
- Object center pixel location
- A bounding box surrounding the object as output
- In instance image where each pixel is classified into a class. The classes are for object as well as background

When we say object detection, we are usually referring to the first and third type of image recognition. Our goal is to estimate class names as well as bounding box surrounding target objects. Before we begin our discussion on object detection techniques, in the next section we shall see why detecting objects is a difficult computer vision task.

Challenges in object detection

In the past, several approaches for object detection were proposed. However, these either perform well in a controlled environment or look for special objects in images like a human face. Even in the case of faces, the approaches suffer from issues like low light conditions, a highly occluded face or tiny face size compared to the image size.

Following are several challenges that are faced by an object detector in real-world applications:

- **Occlusion**: Objects like dogs or cats can be hidden behind one another, as a result, the features that can be extracted from them are not strong enough to say that they are an object.

- **Viewpoint changes**: In cases of different viewpoints of an object, the shape may change drastically and hence the features of the object will also change drastically. This causes a detector which is trained to see a given object from one viewpoint to fail on seeing it from other viewpoints. For example, in the case of person detection, if the detector is looking for a head, hands, and legs combination to find a person, will fail if we put the camera overhead to take vertical downward facing images. The only thing that the detector will see are heads and hence the results are drastically reduced.

- **Variation in sizes**: The same object can be far from a camera or near. As a result, the size of objects varies. The detector is therefore required to be size invariant as well as rotation invariant.

- **Non-rigid objects**: If the shape of the object splits into parts or there is a fluid object, it becomes even more challenging to describe them using features.

- **Motion-blur**: If we are detecting a moving body like a car, there might be cases where the camera captured image is blurred. This is another challenge for the object detectors, to provide a correct estimation, and making a detector robust is crucial when deployed in moving robots like self-driving cars or drones.

Dataset and libraries used

In this chapter, we will be using TensorFlow (v1.4.0) and OpenCV as our main library for detection. We show results on custom images. However, any colored image can be used as input for various models. Wherever required, there are links to pre-trained model files in the sections.

Methods for object detection

Object detection is the problem of two steps. First, it should localize an object or multiple objects inside an image. Secondly, it gives out a predicted class for each of the localized objects. There have been several object detection methods that use a sliding window-based approach. One of the popular detection techniques is face detection approach, developed by Viola and Jones[1]. The paper exploited the fact that the human face has strong descriptive features such as regions near eyes which are darker than near the mouth. So there may be a significant difference between the rectangle area surrounding the eyes with respect to the rectangular area near the nose. Using this as one of the several pre-defined patterns of rectangle pairs, their method computed area difference between rectangles in each pattern.

Detecting faces is a two-step process:

- First is to create a classifier with parameters for specific object detection. In our case, it is face detection:

```
face_cascade =
cv2.CascadeClassifier('haarcascades/haarcascade_frontalface_default
.xml')
```

- In second step, for each image, it face detection is done using previously loaded classifier parameters:

```
faces = face_cascade.detectMultiScale(gray)
```

In OpenCV we can code this to detect the face, shown as follows:

```
import numpy as np
import cv2

# create cascaded classifier with pre-learned weights
# For other objects, change the file here
face_cascade =
cv2.CascadeClassifier('haarcascades/haarcascade_frontalface_default.xml')
```

```
cap = cv2.VideoCapture(0)

while(True):
    ret, frame = cap.read()
    if not ret:
        print("No frame captured")
    # frame = cv2.resize(frame, (640, 480))
    gray = cv2.cvtColor(frame, cv2.COLOR_BGR2GRAY)

    # detect face
    faces = face_cascade.detectMultiScale(gray)

    # plot results
    for (x,y,w,h) in faces:
        cv2.rectangle(frame, (x,y), (x+w,y+h), (255,0,0),2)

    cv2.imshow('img',frame)
    if cv2.waitKey(1) & 0xFF == ord('q'):
        break

cap.release()
cv2.destroyAllWindows()
```

Here, we used a file `haarcascade_frontalface_default.xml` which contains classifier parameters available at `https://github.com/opencv/opencv/tree/master/data/haarcascades`. We have to download these cascade classifier files in order to run face detection. Also for detecting other objects like eyes, smiles, and so on, we require similar files for use with OpenCV.

The preceding face detector we saw became popular in several devices ranging from smartphones to digital cameras. However, recent advances in deep learning are creating better face detectors. We will see this in the next few sections on deep learning-based general object detectors.

Deep learning-based object detection

With recent advancements in CNNs and their performance in image classification, it was becoming intuitive to use the similar model style for object detection. This has been proven right, as in the last few years there are better object detectors proposed every year which increases overall accuracy on standard benchmarks. Some of the styles of detectors are already in use in smartphones, robot self-driving cars, and so on.

A generic CNN outputs class probabilities, as in the case of image recognition. But in order to detect objects, these must be modified to output both the class probability as well as bounding box rectangle coordinates and shape. Early CNN-based object detection, computes possible windows from an input image and then computes features using a CNN model for each window. This output of the CNN feature extractor will then tell us if the chosen window is the target object or not. This is slow due to a large computation of each window through the CNN feature extractor. Intuitively, we would like to extract features from images and use those features for object detection. This not only enhances speed for detection but also filters unwanted noise in the image.

There have been several methods proposed to tackle such issues of speed and accuracy in object detection. These are in general divided into two major categories:

- **Two-stage detectors**: Here, the overall process is divided into two major steps, hence the name two-stage detectors. The most popular among these is **Faster R-CNN**. In the next section, we will see a detailed explanation of this method.
- **One-stage detectors**: While two-stage detectors increased accuracy for detection, they were still hard to train and they were slower for several real-time operations. One-stage detectors rectified these issues by making a network in single architecture which predicts faster. One of the popular models of this style is **Single Shot Multibox Detector (SSD)**.

In the following sections, we will see both of these types of detectors with a demo that shows the quality of results from each.

Two-stage detectors

As CNN show their performance in general image classification, researchers used the same CNNs to do better object detection. The initial approaches using deep learning for object detection can be described as two-stage detectors and one of the popular ones is Faster R-CNN by Shaoqing Ren, Kaiming He, Ross Girshick, and Jian Sun 2015 `https://arxiv.org/pdf/1506.01497.pdf`.

The method is divided into two stages:

1. In the first stage, the features are extracted from an image and **Region of Interests (ROI)** are proposed. ROIs consists of a possible box where an object might be in the image.
2. The second stage uses features and ROIs to compute final bounding boxes and class probabilities for each of the boxes. These together constitute the final output.

An overview of Faster-RCNN is as shown in the following figure. An input image is used to extract features and a region proposals. These extracted features and proposals are used together to compute predicted bounding boxes and class probabilities for each box:

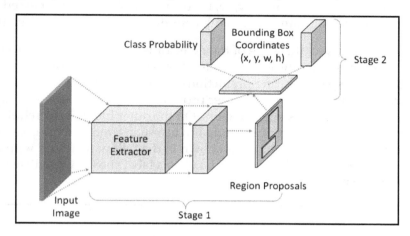

As shown in the previous figure, overall method is considered two-stage because during training the model will first learn to produce ROIs using a sub-model called **Region Proposal Network (RPN)**. It will then learn to produce correct class probabilities and bounding box locations using ROIs and features. An overview of RPN is as shown in the following figure . RPN layer uses feature layer as input creates a proposal for bounding boxes and corresponding probabilities:

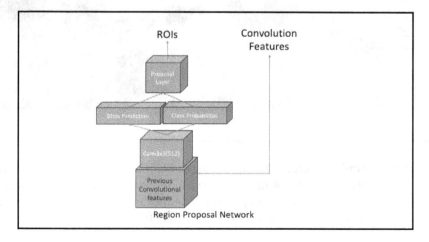

The bounding box locations are usually normalized values for the top left coordinate of the box with width and height values, though this can change depending on the way the model is learnt. During prediction, the model outputs a set of class probabilities, class categories as well as the bounding box location in (x, y, w, h) format. This set is again passed through a threshold to filter out the bounding boxes with confidence scores less than the threshold.

The major advantage of using this style of the detector is that it gives better accuracy than one-stage detectors. These usually achieve state-of-the-art detection accuracy. However, they suffer from slower speeds during predictions. If for an application prediction, time plays a crucial role, then it is advised to either provide these networks with a high-performance system or use one-stage detectors. On the other hand, if the requirement is to get the best accuracy, it is highly recommended to use such a method for object detection. An example output of object detection is as shown in the following figure with the bounding box around detected objects. Each box has a label showing predicted class name and confidence for the box:

The detection in the previous screenshot uses Faster RCNN model and even for small objects, like a person on the right bottom, the model detects with a good confidence score. Overall detected objects are bus, car and person. The model doesn't detect other objects, such as trees, pole, traffic light, and so on because it has not been trained to detect those objects.

Demo – Faster R-CNN with ResNet-101

It can be seen from the previous screenshot that even in the case of varying object sizes and also objects with small sizes, the two-stage model of Faster R-CNN predicts accurately. Now, we will show how to run a similar prediction using TensorFlow. Let's begin by cloning a repository, as it will contain most of the required codes:

```
git clone https://github.com/tensorflow/models.git
cd models/research
```

After we have cloned, we will set up the environment. We will first download a pre-trained model from TensorFlow model-zoo:

- For macOS X:

```
curl -O
http://download.tensorflow.org/models/object_detection/faster_rcnn_
resnet101_coco_2017_11_08.tar.gz
tar -xvf faster_rcnn_resnet101_coco_2017_11_08.tar.gz
```

- For Linux:

```
wget
http://download.tensorflow.org/models/object_detection/faster_rcnn_
resnet101_coco_2017_11_08.gz
tar -xvf faster_rcnn_resnet101_coco_2017_11_08.tar.gz
```

Keep the extracted folder by the name faster_rcnn_resnet101_coco_2017_11_08 in models/research/object_detection. This completes the downloading of the pre-trained model.

These two steps have to be performed each time we launch a Terminal shell:

- At first, we will compile protobuf files, as TensorFlow uses them to serialize structured data:

```
protoc object_detection/protos/*.proto --python_out=.
```

- Also, run in the research folder:

```
export PYTHONPATH=$PYTHONPATH:`pwd`:`pwd`/slim
```

The environment and pre-trained models are set, now we will start with the prediction code. The following code stays and runs inside `models/research/object_detection` and the code style is like a Jupyter notebook. As we progress in this section, each of the further code blocks can be run inside a Jupyter notebook cell. If you are not familiar with Jupyter, you can still run complete Python scripts:

1. Let's begin with loading libs that will be used here:

```
import numpy as np
import os
import sys
import tensorflow as tf
import cv2
from matplotlib import pyplot as plt
# inside jupyter uncomment next line
# %matplotlib inline
import random
import time
from utils import label_map_util
```

2. In order to load a pre-trained model for prediction:

```
# load graph
def load_and_create_graph(path_to_pb):
    """
    Loads pre-trained graph from .pb file.
    path_to_pb: path to saved .pb file
    Tensorflow keeps graph global so nothing is returned
    """
    with tf.gfile.FastGFile(path_to_pb, 'rb') as f:
        # initialize graph definition
        graph_def = tf.GraphDef()
        # reads file
        graph_def.ParseFromString(f.read())
        # imports as tf.graph
        _ = tf.import_graph_def(graph_def, name='')
```

3. It can be used to load the model Faster R-CNN with the ResNet-101 feature extractor pre-trained on MSCOCO dataset:

```
load_and_create_graph('faster_rcnn_resnet101_coco_2017_11_08/frozen
_inference_graph.pb')
```

4. Now, let's set up labels to display in our figure using MSCOCO labels:

```
# load labels for classes output
path_to_labels = os.path.join('data', 'mscoco_label_map.pbtxt')
# pre-training was done on 90 categories
nb_classes = 90
label_map = label_map_util.load_labelmap(path_to_labels)
categories =
label_map_util.convert_label_map_to_categories(label_map,
                    max_num_classes=nb_classes,
use_display_name=True)
category_index = label_map_util.create_category_index(categories)
```

5. Before final predictions, we will set up the utility function as:

```
def read_cv_image(filename):
    """
    Reads an input color image and converts to RGB order
    Returns image as an array
    """
    img = cv2.imread(filename)
    img = cv2.cvtColor(img, cv2.COLOR_BGR2RGB)
    return img
```

6. Following is utility function to display bounding boxes using matplotlib:

```
def show_mpl_img_with_detections(img, dets, scores,
                                 classes, category_index,
                                 thres=0.6):
    """
    Applies thresholding to each box score and
    plot bbox results on image.
    img: input image as numpy array
    dets: list of K detection outputs for given image.(size:[1,K])
    scores: list of detection score for each detection output(size:
[1,K]).
    classes: list of predicted class index(size: [1,K])
    category_index: dictionary containing mapping from class index
to class name.
    thres: threshold to filter detection boxes:(default: 0.6)
    By default K:100 detections
    """
    # plotting utilities from matplotlib
    plt.figure(figsize=(12,8))
    plt.imshow(img)
    height = img.shape[0]
```

```
        width = img.shape[1]
        # To use common color of one class and different for different
classes
        colors = dict()
        # iterate over all proposed bbox
        # choose whichever is more than a threshold
        for i in range(dets.shape[0]):
            cls_id = int(classes[i])
            # in case of any wrong prediction for class index
            if cls_id >= 0:
                score = scores[i]
                # score for a detection is more than a threshold
                if score > thres:
                    if cls_id not in colors:
                        colors[cls_id] = (random.random(),
                                          random.random(),
                                          random.random())
                    xmin = int(dets[i, 1] * width)
                    ymin = int(dets[i, 0] * height)
                    xmax = int(dets[i, 3] * width)
                    ymax = int(dets[i, 2] * height)
                    rect = plt.Rectangle((xmin, ymin), xmax - xmin,
                                         ymax - ymin, fill=False,
                                         edgecolor=colors[cls_id],
                                         linewidth=2.5)
                    plt.gca().add_patch(rect)
                    # to plot class name and score around each
detection box
                    class_name = str(category_index[cls_id]['name'])
                    plt.gca().text(xmin, ymin - 2,
                            '{:s} {:.3f}'.format(class_name, score),
                            bbox=dict(facecolor=colors[cls_id],
alpha=0.5),
                            fontsize=8, color='white')
    plt.axis('off')
    plt.show()

    return
```

Using this setup, we can do predictions on the input image. In the following snippet, we are doing predictions on the input image as well as displaying the results. We will launch a `Tensorflow` session and run the graph in `sess.run` to compute bounding boxes, scores for each box, the class prediction for boxes and number of detections:

```
image_dir = 'test_images/'
# create graph object from previously loaded graph
# tensorflow previously loaded graph as default
graph=tf.get_default_graph()

# launch a session to run this graph
with tf.Session(graph=graph) as sess:
    # get input node
    image_tensor = graph.get_tensor_by_name('image_tensor:0')
    # get output nodes
    detection_boxes = graph.get_tensor_by_name('detection_boxes:0')
    detection_scores = graph.get_tensor_by_name('detection_scores:0')
    detection_classes = graph.get_tensor_by_name('detection_classes:0')
    num_detections = graph.get_tensor_by_name('num_detections:0')
    # read image from file and pre-process it for input.
    # Note: we can do this outside session scope too.
    image = read_cv_image(os.path.join(image_dir, 'cars2.png'))
    input_img = image[np.newaxis, :, :, :]
    # To compute prediction time
    start = time.time()
    # Run prediction and get 4 outputs
    (boxes, scores, classes, num) = sess.run(
        [detection_boxes, detection_scores, detection_classes,
num_detections],
        feed_dict={image_tensor: input_img})
    end = time.time()
    print("Prediction time:",end-start,"secs for ", num[0], "detections")
    # display results
    show_mpl_img_with_detections(image, boxes[0],scores[0],
classes[0],category_index, thres=0.6)
```

Using previous code, an example of prediction is as shown in the following screenshot. Each detected object is displayed with the bounding box. Each bounding box has a name of the predicted class as well as the confidence score for the object inside the box:

One-stage detectors

In the previous section, we saw that two-stage detectors suffer from the issue of slower prediction time and harder training by splitting the network into two. In recently proposed networks like **Single Shot Multibox Detectors (SSD)**[3], the prediction time is reduced by removing the intermediate stage and the training is always end-to-end. These networks have shown effectiveness by running on smartphones as well as low-end computation units:

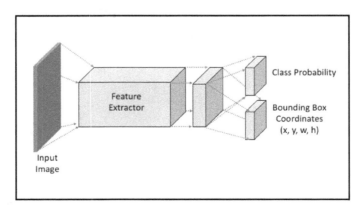

An abstract view of the network is shown in the preceding figure. The overall output of the network is same as two-stage, the class probability for the object and bounding box coordinates of the form (**x, y, w, h**), where (x,y) is the top-left corner of the rectangle and (w, h) are the width and height of the box respectively. In order to use multiple resolutions, the model not only uses the final layer of feature extraction but also several intermediate feature layers. An abstract view is shown in the following screenshot:

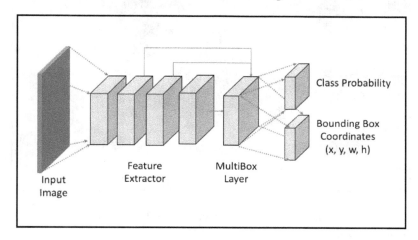

To further increase the speed for detection, the model also uses a technique called **non-maximal suppression**. This will suppress all the **Bounding Box** which do not have a maximum score in a given region and for a given category. As a result, the total output boxes from the **MultiBox Layer** are reduced significantly and thus we have only high scored detections per class in an image.

In the next section, we will see TensorFlow-based SSD object detection. We will use some of the code from the previous section; Reader does not need to install again if there is already an installation of the previous section.

Demo

In the following codes, we will load a pre-trained model and perform an object detection task on pre-defined 90 categories. Before we begin, check that there is a working TensorFlow (Version = 1.4.0) Python environment.

In this section, our input is as shown in the image with people:

We will follow similar instructions as that of two-stage detectors and begin by cloning TensorFlow/models repo:

```
git clone https://github.com/tensorflow/models.git
cd models/research
```

Let's download a pre-trained model from TensorFlow model-zoo. These are for one-stage detectors:

- For macOS X:

```
curl -O
http://download.tensorflow.org/models/object_detection/ssd_inceptio
n_v2_coco_2017_11_17.tar.gz
tar -xvf ssd_inception_v2_coco_2017_11_17.tar.gz
```

- For Linux:

```
wget
http://download.tensorflow.org/models/object_detection/ssd_inceptio
n_v2_coco_2017_11_17.tar.gz
tar -xvf ssd_inception_v2_coco_2017_11_17.tar.gz
```

Similarly, keep the extracted folder by the name `ssd_inception_v2_coco_2017_11_17` in `models/research/object_detection`. We will set up the environment now. If this has already been done from the previous section, please skip this:

- First, we will compile the `protobuf` files:

```
protoc object_detection/protos/*.proto --python_out=.
```

- Also, run in the research folder:

```
export PYTHONPATH=$PYTHONPATH:`pwd`:`pwd`/slim
```

Let's begin with loading libraries:

```
import numpy as np
import os
import sys
import tensorflow as tf
import cv2
from matplotlib import pyplot as plt
# inside jupyter uncomment next line
# %matplotlib inline
import random
import time
from utils import label_map_util
```

1. The following code reads pre-trained model. In TensorFlow, these models are usually saved as `protobuf` in `.pb` format. Also, note that if there are other formats of pre-trained model files, then we may have to read accordingly:

```
def load_and_create_graph(path_to_pb):
    """
    Loads pre-trained graph from .pb file.
    path_to_pb: path to saved .pb file
    Tensorflow keeps graph global so nothing is returned
    """
    with tf.gfile.FastGFile(path_to_pb, 'rb') as f:
        # initialize graph definition
        graph_def = tf.GraphDef()
        # reads file
        graph_def.ParseFromString(f.read())
        # imports as tf.graph
        _ = tf.import_graph_def(graph_def, name='')
```

2. For using our input image, the following block reads an image from a given path to a file:

```
def read_cv_image(filename):
    """
    Reads an input color image and converts to RGB order
    Returns image as an array
    """
    img = cv2.imread(filename)
    img = cv2.cvtColor(img, cv2.COLOR_BGR2RGB)
    return img
```

3. The last utility function is for the output display of the bounding box around the predicted object with the class name and detection score for each box:

```
def show_mpl_img_with_detections(img, dets, scores,
                                 classes, category_index,
                                 thres=0.6):
    """
    Applies thresholding to each box score and
    plot bbox results on image.
    img: input image as numpy array
    dets: list of K detection outputs for given image. (size:[1,K]
)
    scores: list of detection score for each detection output(size:
[1,K]).
    classes: list of predicted class index(size: [1,K])
    category_index: dictionary containing mapping from class index
to class name.
    thres: threshold to filter detection boxes:(default: 0.6)
    By default K:100 detections
    """
    # plotting utilities from matplotlib
    plt.figure(figsize=(12,8))
    plt.imshow(img)
    height = img.shape[0]
    width = img.shape[1]
    # To use common color of one class and different for different
classes
    colors = dict()
    # iterate over all proposed bbox
    # choose whichever is more than a threshold
    for i in range(dets.shape[0]):
        cls_id = int(classes[i])
        # in case of any wrong prediction for class index
        if cls_id >= 0:
            score = scores[i]
```

```
                    # score for a detection is more than a threshold
                    if score > thres:
                        if cls_id not in colors:
                            colors[cls_id] = (random.random(),
                                              random.random(),
                                              random.random())
                        xmin = int(dets[i, 1] * width)
                        ymin = int(dets[i, 0] * height)
                        xmax = int(dets[i, 3] * width)
                        ymax = int(dets[i, 2] * height)
                        rect = plt.Rectangle((xmin, ymin), xmax - xmin,
                                             ymax - ymin, fill=False,
                                             edgecolor=colors[cls_id],
                                             linewidth=2.5)
                        plt.gca().add_patch(rect)
                        # to plot class name and score around each
    detection box
                        class_name = str(category_index[cls_id]['name'])
                        plt.gca().text(xmin, ymin - 2,
                                       '{:s} {:.3f}'.format(class_name, score),
                                       bbox=dict(facecolor=colors[cls_id],
    alpha=0.5),
                                       fontsize=8, color='white')
            plt.axis('off')
            plt.show()

        return
```

4. We will be using an SSD model for object detection that uses Inception-v2 model
   for feature extraction. This model is pre-trained on the MSCOCO dataset. We saw
   earlier the code snippet to download the model and also to load. So let's go ahead
   and read the model:

```
# load pre-trained model
load_and_create_graph('ssd_inception_v2_coco_2017_11_17/frozen_infe
rence_graph.pb')
```

5. Before we start using the model to do predictions on the input image, we need
   our output to make sense. We will create a dictionary map of the class index to
   pre-defined class names. The following code will read a file
   data/mscoco_label_map.pbtxt which contains this index to class name
   mapping. The final index can be used to read our output as class names:

```
# load labels for classes output
path_to_labels = os.path.join('data', 'mscoco_label_map.pbtxt')
nb_classes = 90
```

```
label_map = label_map_util.load_labelmap(path_to_labels)
categories =
label_map_util.convert_label_map_to_categories(label_map,
                    max_num_classes=nb_classes,
use_display_name=True)
category_index = label_map_util.create_category_index(categories)
```

We have set up everything necessary for prediction. In TensorFlow, the model is represented as a computational graph and is often referred to as graph in code snippets. This consists of various layers and operation on layers represented as a node the and connection between them is how the data will flow. For performing predictions, we need to know the input node name and output node names. There can be more than one nodes of a type. To start performing the computation, we will first create a session. A graph can only perform computation inside a session and we can create a session as we need it in the program. In the following code snippet, we create a session and get pre-defined input node and output nodes:

```
image_dir = 'test_images/'
# create graph object from previously loaded graph
# tensorflow previously loaded graph as default
graph=tf.get_default_graph()

# launch a session to run this graph
with tf.Session(graph=graph) as sess:
    # get input node
    image_tensor = graph.get_tensor_by_name('image_tensor:0')
    # get output nodes
    detection_boxes = graph.get_tensor_by_name('detection_boxes:0')
    detection_scores = graph.get_tensor_by_name('detection_scores:0')
    detection_classes = graph.get_tensor_by_name('detection_classes:0')
    num_detections = graph.get_tensor_by_name('num_detections:0')
    # read image from file and pre-process it for input.
    # Note: we can do this outside session scope too.
    image = read_cv_image(os.path.join(image_dir, 'person1.png'))
    # Input Shape : [N, Width,Height,Channels],
    # where N=1, batch size
    input_img = image[np.newaxis, :, :, :]
    # To compute prediction time
    start = time.time()
    # Run prediction and get 4 outputs
    (boxes, scores, classes, num) = sess.run(
            [detection_boxes, detection_scores, detection_classes,
num_detections],
            feed_dict={image_tensor: input_img})
    end = time.time()
    print("Prediction time:",end-start,"secs for ", num, "detections")
```

```
# display results with score threshold of 0.6
# Since only one image is used , hence we use 0 index for outputs
show_mpl_img_with_detections(image, boxes[0],scores[0], classes[0],
thres=0.6)
```

In the previous code, the input node is `image_tensor:0` and four output nodes
are `detection_boxes:0`, `detection_scores:0`, `detection_classes:0`,
and `num_detections:0`.

When we run inference on a given image, the inference is as shown in the following figure.
Each box color is according to the class, and the predicted class name, as well as the score
for class prediction, is displayed in the top-left corner. Ideally, score one shows the model is
100% sure about the category of an object inside the box:

> This score is not for how correct the box is but only for the confidence for
> the category of the object inside.

Here we used only one image as input. We can use a list of images as input and correspondingly we will get a list of outputs for each image. To display the results, iterate simultaneously on images and outputs as follows:

```
for i in range(nb_inputs):
    show_mpl_img_with_detections(images[i], boxes[i],scores[i], classes[i],
thres=0.6)
```

To show the comparison with the two-stage detector, for the same input the following are the output prediction with the one-stage detector. We can easily notice that the one-stage detectors such as SSD is good for large objects but fail to recognize small objects such as people. Also, the prediction scores vary a lot between the two detectors:

Summary

This chapter gives an overview of object detection and several challenges in modeling a good detector. While there are many methods for detection using deep learning, common categories are one-stage and two-stage detectors. Each of the detectors has its own advantages, such as one-stage detectors are good for real-time applications while two-stage detectors are good for high accuracy output. The difference in accuracy between the models is shown using example figures. We can now understand the choice of object detector and run a pre-trained model using TensorFlow. The various output samples for each show the effectiveness of models in complex images.

In the next chapter, we will learn more about the image recognition problems of segmentation as well as tracking using deep learning methods.

References

- Viola Paul and Michael J. Jones. *Robust real-time face detection*. International journal of computer vision 57, no. 2 (2004): 137-154.
- Ren Shaoqing, Kaiming He, Ross Girshick, and Jian Sun. *Faster R-CNN: Towards real-time object detection with region proposal networks*. In Advances in neural information processing systems, pp. 91-99. 2015.
- Liu Wei, Dragomir Anguelov, Dumitru Erhan, Christian Szegedy, Scott Reed, Cheng-Yang Fu, and Alexander C. Berg. *SSD: Single Shot Multibox Detector*. In European conference on computer vision, pp. 21-37. Springer, Cham, 2016.
- Lin et al., *Microsoft COCO: Common Objects in Context*, `https://arxiv.org/pdf/1405.0312.pdf`.

7
Segmentation and Tracking

In the previous chapter, we studied different methods for feature extraction and image classification using **Convolutional Neural Networks** (**CNNs**) to detect objects in an image. Those methods work well in creating a bounding box around the target object. However, if our application requires a precise boundary, called an **instance**, around the object, we need to apply a different approach.

In this chapter, we will be focusing on object instance detection, which is also termed image segmentation. In the second part of the chapter, we will first see MOSSE tracker with OpenCV see various approaches to tracking objects in a sequence of image

Segmentation and tracking are, however, not quite interlinked problems, but they depend heavily on the previous approaches of feature extraction and object detection. The application's range is quite vast, including image editing, image denoising, surveillance, motion capture, and so on. The chosen methods for segmentation and tracking are suitable for specific applications.

Datasets and libraries

We will be continuing the use of OpenCV and NumPy for image processing. For deep learning, we will use Keras with the TensorFlow backend. For segmentation, we will be using the `Pascal VOC` dataset. This has annotations for object detection, as well as segmentation. For tracking, we will use the `MOT16` dataset, which consists of an annotated sequence of images from video. We will mention how to use the code in the sections where it is used.

Segmentation

Segmentation is often referred to as the clustering of pixels of a similar category. An example is as shown in the following screenshot. Here, we see that inputs are on the left and the segmentation results are on the right. The colors of an object are according to pre-defined object categories. These examples are taken from the `Pascal VOC` dataset:

In the top picture on the left, there are several small aeroplanes in the background and, therefore, we see small pixels colored accordingly in the corresponding image on the right. In the bottom-left picture, there are two pets laying together, therefore, their segmented image on the right has different colors for the pixels belonging to the cat and dog respectively. In this figure, the boundary is differently colored for convenience and does not imply a different category.

In traditional segmentation techniques, the key property used is image intensity levels. First, different smaller regions of similar intensity values are found, and later they are merged into larger regions. To get the best performance, an initial point is chosen by the user for algorithms. Recent approaches using deep learning have shown better performance without the need for initialization. In further sections, we will see an extension of previously seen CNNs for image segmentation.

Before starting our discussion on segmentation methods, let's look at the challenges.

Challenges in segmentation

The challenges in a segmentation task are greater than the previous object detection task, as the complexity of detection is increased:

- **Noisy boundaries**: Grouping pixels that belong to a category may not be as accurate due to the fuzzy edges of an object. As a result, objects from different categories are clustered together.
- **Cluttered scene**: With several objects in the image frame, it becomes harder to classify pixels correctly. With more clutter, the chances of false positive classification also increase.

CNNs for segmentation

Deep learning based segmentation approaches have recently grown, both in terms of accuracy as well as effectiveness, in more complex domains. One of the popular models using CNN for segmentation is a **fully convolutional network (FCN)**[5], which we will explore in this section. This method has the advantage of training an end-to-end CNN to perform pixel-wise semantic segmentation. The output is an image with each pixel classified as either background or into one of the predefined categories of objects. The overall architecture is shown in the following screenshot:

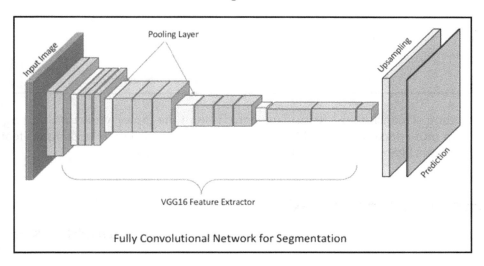

As the layers are stacked hierarchically, the output from each layer gets downsampled yet is feature rich. In the last layer, as shown in the figure, the downsampled output is upsampled using a deconvolutional layer, resulting in the final output being the same size as that of the input.

The deconvolutional layer is used to transform the input feature to the upsampled feature, however, the name is a bit misleading, as the operation is not exactly the inverse of convolution. This acts as transposed convolution, where the input is convolved after a transpose, as compared to a regular convolution operation.

In the previous model, the upsampling of the feature layer was done with a single layer. This can, however, be extended over to a hierarchical structure, as follows:

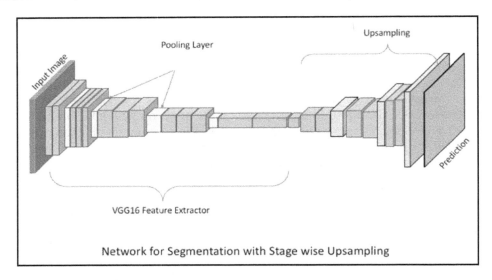

Network for Segmentation with Stage wise Upsampling

In the preceding screenshot, the feature extractor is kept the same, while upsampling is updated with more deconvolutional layers where each of these layers upsamples features from the previous layer and generates an overall richer prediction.

Implementation of FCN

In this section, we will learn to model one of the basic segmentation models in Keras.

Let's begin by importing Keras required modules:

```
from keras.models import *
from keras.layers import *
from keras.applications.vgg16 import VGG16
```

The following code will create an FCN model, which takes in VGG16 features as input and adds further layers for fine tuning them. These are then upsampled to give resulting output:

```
def create_model_fcn32(nb_class, input_w=256):
    """
    Create FCN-32s model for segmentaiton.
    Input:
        nb_class: number of detection categories
        input_w: input width, using square image

    Returns model created for training.
    """
    input = Input(shape=(input_w, input_w, 3))

    # initialize feature extractor excuding fully connected layers
    # here we use VGG model, with pre-trained weights.
    vgg = VGG16(include_top=False, weights='imagenet', input_tensor=input)
    # create further network
    x = Conv2D(4096, kernel_size=(7,7), use_bias=False,
                activation='relu', padding="same")(vgg.output)
    x = Dropout(0.5)(x)
    x = Conv2D(4096, kernel_size=(1,1), use_bias=False,
                activation='relu', padding="same")(x)
    x = Dropout(0.5)(x)
    x = Conv2D(nb_class, kernel_size=(1,1), use_bias=False,
                padding="same")(x)
    # upsampling to image size using transposed convolution layer
    x = Conv2DTranspose(nb_class ,
                        kernel_size=(64,64),
                        strides=(32,32),
                        use_bias=False, padding='same')(x)
    x = Activation('softmax')(x)
    model = Model(input, x)
    model.summary()
    return model

# Create model for pascal voc image segmentation for 21 classes
model = create_model_fcn32(21)
```

In this section, we saw segmentation methods to compute object precise region in an image. The FCN method shown here uses only convolutional layers to compute these regions. The `upsampling` method is key to compute pixel-wise categories and hence different choices of upsampling methods will result in a different quality of results.

Tracking

Tracking is the problem of estimating the position of an object over consecutive image sequences. This is also further divided into single object tracking and multiple object tracking, however, both single and multi-object tracking require slightly different approaches. In this section, we will see the methods for multi-object tracking, as well as single-object tracking.

The methods for image-based tracking are used in several applications, such as action recognition, self-driving cars, security and surveillance, augmented reality apps, motion capture systems, and video compression techniques. In **Augmented Reality** (**AR**) apps, for example, if we want to draw a virtual three-dimensional object on a planar surface, we would want to keep track of the planar surface for a feasible output.

In surveillance or traffic monitoring, tracking vehicles and keeping records of number plates helps to manage traffic and keeps security in check. Also, in video compression applications, if we already know that a single object is the only thing changing in frames, we can perform better compression by using only those pixels that change, thereby optimizing video transmission and receiving.

In the setup of tracking, we will first see challenges in the next section.

Challenges in tracking

It is always crucial to know which challenges we need to take care of before building apps. As a standard computer vision method, a lot of the challenges here are common:

- **Object occlusion**: If the target object is hidden behind other objects in a sequence of images, then it becomes not only hard to detect the object but also to update future images if it becomes visible again.
- **Fast movement**: Cameras, such as on smartphones, often suffers from jittery movement. This causes a blurring effect and, sometimes, the complete absence of an object from the frame. Therefore, sudden changes in the motion of cameras also lead to problems in tracking applications.

- **Change of shape**: If we are targeting non-rigid objects, changes in shape or the complete deformation of an object will often lead to being unable to detect the object and also tracking failure.
- **False positives**: In a scene with multiple similar objects, it is hard to match which object is targeted in subsequent images. The tracker may lose the current object in terms of detection and start tracking a similar object.

These challenges can make our applications crash suddenly or give a completely incorrect estimate of an object's location.

Methods for object tracking

An intuitive method for tracking is to use the object detection method from the previous chapter and compute detection in each frame. This will result in a bounding box detection for every frame, but we would also like to know if a particular object stays in the image sequence and for how many frames, that is, to keep track of K-frames for the object in the scene. We would also need a matching strategy to say that the object found in the previous image is the same as the one in the current image frame.

Continuing with this intuition, we add a predictor for the bounding box motion. We assume a state for the bounding box, which consists of coordinates for the box center as well as its velocities. This state changes as we see more boxes in the sequence.

Given the current state of the box, we can predict a possible region for where it will be in the next frame by assuming some noise in our measurement. The object detector can search for an object similar to the previous object in the next possible region. The location of the newly found object box and the previous box state will help us to update the new state of the box. This will be used for the next frame. As a result, iterating this process over all of the frames will result in not only the tracking of the object bounding box but keeping a location check on particular objects over the whole sequence. This method of tracking is also termed as **tracking by detection.**

In tracking by detection, each frame uses an object detector to find possible instances of objects and matches those detections with corresponding objects in the previous frame.

On the other hand, if no object detector is to be used, we can initialize the target object and track it by matching it and finding a similar object in each frame.

In the following section, we will see two popular methods for tracking. The first method is quite fast, yet simple, while the latter is quite accurate, even in the case of multiple-object tracking.

MOSSE tracker

This is proposed by for fast object tracking using correlation filter methods. Correlation filter-based tracking comprises the following steps:

1. Assuming a template of a target object T and an input image I, we first take the **Fast Fourier Transform** (**FFT**) of both the template (T) and the image (I).
2. A convolution operation is performed between template T and image I.
3. The result from step 2 is inverted to the spatial domain using **Inverse Fast Fourier Transform** (**IFFT**). The position of the template object in the image I is the max value of the IFFT response we get.

This correlation filter-based technique has limitations in the choice of T. As a single template image match may not observe all the variations of an object, such as rotation in the image sequence, Bolme, and its co-authors[1] proposed a more robust tracker-based correlation filter, termed as **Minimum Output Sum of Squared Error** (**MOSSE**) filter. In this method, the template T for matching is first learned by minimizing a sum of squared error as:

$$\min_{T^*} \sum_i |I_i \odot T^* - O_i|^2$$

Here, i is the training samples and the resulting learned template is T^*.

 We will see the implementation of MOSSE tracker from OpenCV, as it already has good implementation here: https://github.com/opencv/opencv/blob/master/samples/python/mosse.py

We will look at the key parts of the following code:

```python
def correlate(self, img):
    """
    Correlation of input image with the kernel
    """

    # get response in fourier domain
    C = cv2.mulSpectrums(cv2.dft(img, flags=cv2.DFT_COMPLEX_OUTPUT),
                         self.H, 0, conjB=True)

    # compute inverse to get image domain output
    resp = cv2.idft(C, flags=cv2.DFT_SCALE | cv2.DFT_REAL_OUTPUT)
    # max location of the response
    h, w = resp.shape
```

```
_, mval, _, (mx, my) = cv2.minMaxLoc(resp)
side_resp = resp.copy()
cv2.rectangle(side_resp, (mx-5, my-5), (mx+5, my+5), 0, -1)
smean, sstd = side_resp.mean(), side_resp.std()
psr = (mval-smean) / (sstd+eps)

# displacement of max location from center is displacement for
tracker
return resp, (mx-w//2, my-h//2), psr
```

The update function gets a frame from video or image sequence iteratively and updates the state of the tracker:

```
def update(self, frame, rate = 0.125):
        # compute current state and window size
        (x, y), (w, h) = self.pos, self.size
        # compute and update rectangular area from new frame
        self.last_img = img = cv2.getRectSubPix(frame, (w, h), (x, y))
        # pre-process it by normalization
        img = self.preprocess(img)
        # apply correlation and compute displacement
        self.last_resp, (dx, dy), self.psr = self.correlate(img)
        self.good = self.psr > 8.0
        if not self.good:
            return

        # update pos
        self.pos = x+dx, y+dy
        self.last_img = img = cv2.getRectSubPix(frame, (w, h), self.pos)
        img = self.preprocess(img)

        A = cv2.dft(img, flags=cv2.DFT_COMPLEX_OUTPUT)
        H1 = cv2.mulSpectrums(self.G, A, 0, conjB=True)
        H2 = cv2.mulSpectrums( A, A, 0, conjB=True)
        self.H1 = self.H1 * (1.0-rate) + H1 * rate
        self.H2 = self.H2 * (1.0-rate) + H2 * rate
        self.update_kernel()
```

A major advantage of using the MOSSE filter is that it is quite fast for real-time tracking systems. The overall algorithm is simple to implement and can be used in the hardware without special image processing libraries, such as embedded platforms. There have been several modifications to this filter and, as such, readers are requested to explore more about these filters.

Deep SORT

Previously, we looked at one of the simplest trackers. In this section, we will use richer features from CNNs to perform tracking. **Deep SORT**[2] is a recent algorithm for tracking that extends **Simple Online and Real-time Tracking**[3] and has shown remarkable results in the **Multiple Object Tracking (MOT)** problem.

In the problem setting of MOT, each frame has more than one object to track. A generic method to solve this has two steps:

- **Detection**: First, all the objects are detected in the frame. There can be single or multiple detections.
- **Association**: Once we have detections for the frame, a matching is performed for similar detections with respect to the previous frame. The matched frames are followed through the sequence to get the tracking for an object.

In Deep SORT, this generic method is further divided into three steps:

1. To compute detections, a popular CNN-based object detection method is used. In the paper[2], Faster-RCNN[4] is used to perform the initial detection per frame. As explained in the previous chapter, this method is two-stage object detection, which performs well for object detection, even in cases of object transformations and occlusions.
2. The intermediate step before data association consists of an estimation model. This uses the state of each track as a vector of eight quantities, that is, box center (x, y), box scale (s), box aspect ratio (a), and their derivatives with time as velocities. The Kalman filter is used to model these states as a dynamical system. If there is no detection of a tracking object for a threshold of consecutive frames, it is considered to be out of frame or lost. For a newly detected box, the new track is started.

3. In the final step, given the predicted states from Kalman filtering using the previous information and the newly detected box in the current frame, an association is made for the new detection with old object tracks in the previous frame. This is computed using Hungarian algorithm on bipartite graph matching. This is made even more robust by setting the weights of the matching with distance formulation.

This is further explained in the following diagram. The tracker uses a vector of states to store the historical information for previous detections. If a new frame comes, we can either use pre-stores bounding box detections or compute them using object detection methods discussed in *chapter 6*. Finally, using current observation of bounding box detections and previous states, the current tracking is estimated:

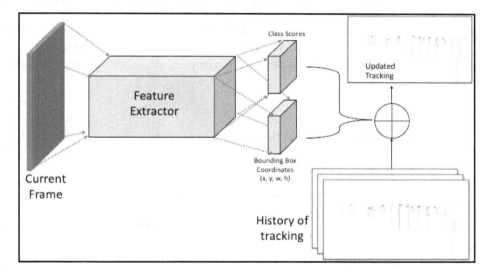

We will see an effective demo of Deep SORT using its official repository at `https://github.com/nwojke/deep_sort`

At first, clone the following repository:

```
git clone https://github.com/nwojke/deep_sort.git
```

Since we already have TensorFlow and Keras installed, we will not be going through their installation. As we saw previously, it uses CNN-based object detection for initial detection. We can run the network and get detection or use pre-generated detections. To do so, let's get pre-trained models here in the `deep_sort` folder:

- On macOS (if `wget` is not available):

  ```
  curl -O
  https://owncloud.uni-koblenz.de/owncloud/s/f9JB0Jr7f3zzqs8/download
  ```

- On Linux:

  ```
  wget
  https://owncloud.uni-koblenz.de/owncloud/s/f9JB0Jr7f3zzqs8/download
  ```

These downloaded files consist of pre-detected boxes using CNN-based models for the MOT challenge dataset CC BY-NC-SA 3.0. We need one more thing to use the downloaded model, that is, a dataset on which these detections were created. Let's get the dataset from `https://motchallenge.net/data/MOT16.zip`:

- On macOS:

  ```
  curl -O https://motchallenge.net/data/MOT16.zip
  ```

- On Linux:

  ```
  wget https://motchallenge.net/data/MOT16.zip
  ```

Now that we have finished setting up the code structure, we can run a demo:

```
python deep_sort_app.py \
    --sequence_dir=./MOT16/test/MOT16-06 \
    --
detection_file=./deep_sort_data/resources/detections/MOT16_POI_test/MOT16-0
6.npy \
    --min_confidence=0.3 \
    --display=True
```

In this case:

- `--sequence_dir` is the path to the MOT challenge test image sequence
- `--detection_file` is our downloaded pre-generated detection corresponding to the sequence directory we chose previously
- `--min_confidence` is the threshold to filter any detection less than this value

For test sequence MOT16-06, we can see the window which shows video output frame-by-frame. Each frame consists of the bounding box around person tracked and the number is the ID of the person being tracked. The number updates if a new person is detected and follows until the tracking stops. In the following figure, a sample output is explained from the tracking window. For ease of explanation, background image is not shown and only tracking boxes are shown:

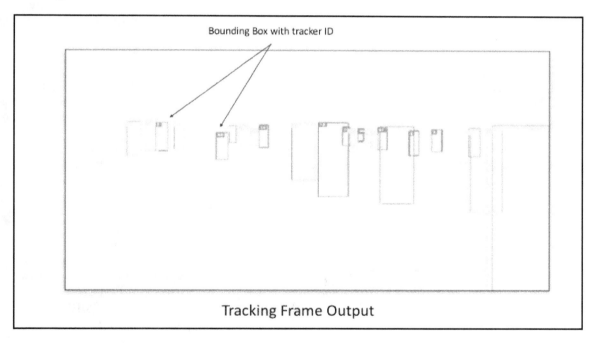

Tracking Frame Output

Readers are encourages to run other test sequences too, like MOT16-07, to further understand effectiveness of the model with varying environments.

In this section, we saw a demo of the Deep SORT method for MOT. One of the crucial parts of this method is detection and the use of Faster RCNN as a good detector. However, to increase the speed of the overall algorithm, Faster RCNN can also be replaced by other fast object detectors such as the Single Shot detector, because the rest of the method uses detected box states and not on the feature extraction method and features itself.

Summary

In this chapter, two different computer vision problems were shown. In segmentation, both the pixel level as well as convolutional neural net-based methods were shown. FCN shows the effectiveness of segmenting an image using the feature extraction method and, as a result, several current applications can be based on it. In track, two different approaches were discussed. Tracking by detection and tracking by matching can both be used for applications to track objects in the video. MOSSE tracker is a simple tracker for fast-paced applications and can be implemented on small computing devices. The Deep SORT method explained in this chapter can be used for multi-object tracking that uses deep CNN object detectors.

In the next chapter, we will begin with another branch of computer vision that focuses on understanding geometry of the scene explicitly. We will see methods to compute camera position and track its trajectory using only images.

References

- Bolme David S. J. Ross Beveridge, Bruce A. Draper, and Yui Man Lui. *Visual object tracking using adaptive correlation filters*. In Computer Vision and Pattern Recognition (CVPR), 2010 IEEE Conference on, pp. 2544-2550. IEEE, 2010.
- Wojke, Nicolai, Alex Bewley, and Dietrich Paulus. *Simple Online and Realtime Tracking with a Deep Association Metric*. arXiv preprint arXiv:1703.07402 (2017).

- Bewley, Alex, Zongyuan Ge, Lionel Ott, Fabio Ramos, and Ben Upcroft. *Simple online and realtime tracking.* In Image Processing (ICIP), 2016 IEEE International Conference on, pp. 3464-3468. IEEE, 2016.
- Ren, Shaoqing, Kaiming He, Ross Girshick, and Jian Sun. *Faster R-CNN: Towards real-time object detection with region proposal networks.* In Advances in neural information processing systems, pp. 91-99. 2015.
- Long, Jonathan, Evan Shelhamer, and Trevor Darrell. *Fully convolutional networks for semantic segmentation.* In Proceedings of the IEEE Conference on Computer Vision and Pattern Recognition, pp. 3431-3440. 2015.

3D Computer Vision

8

In the last few chapters, we have discussed the extraction of an object and semantic information from images. We saw how good feature extraction leads to object detection, segmentation, and tracking. This information explicitly requires the geometry of the scene; in several applications, knowing the exact geometry of a scene plays a vital role.

In this chapter, we will see a discussion leading to the three-dimensional aspects of an image. Here, we will begin by using a simple camera model to understand how pixel values and real-world points are linked correspondingly. Later, we will study methods for computing depth from images and also methods of computing the motion of a camera from a sequence of images.

We will cover the following topics in the chapter:

- RGDB dataset
- Applications to extract features from images
- Image formation
- Aligning of images
- Visual odometry
- Visual SLAM

Dataset and libraries

In this chapter, we will be using OpenCV for most of the applications. In the last section, for **Visual Simultaneous Localization and Mapping (vSLAM)** techniques, we will see the use of an open source repository; directions for its use are mentioned in the section. The dataset is the RGBD dataset, consisting of a sequence of images captured using RGB and a depth camera. To download this dataset, visit the following link and download the **fr1/xyz** tar file: https://vision.in.tum.de/data/datasets/rgbd-dataset/download.

Alternatively, use the following (Linux only) command in a Terminal:

```
wget
https://vision.in.tum.de/rgbd/dataset/freiburg1/rgbd_dataset_freiburg1_xyz.
tgz
tar -xvf rgbd_dataset_freiburg1_xyz.tgz
```

Applications

While deep learning can extract good features for high-level applications, there are areas that require pixel level matching to compute geometric information from an image. Some of the applications that use this information are:

- **Drones**: In commercial robots like drones, the image sequence is used to compute the motion of the camera mounted on them. This helps them to make robust motion estimations and, in addition to other **Inertial Measurement Units (IMU)** such as gyroscopes, accelerometers, and so on, the overall motion is estimated more accurately.
- **Image editing applications**: Smartphones and professional applications for image editing include tools like panorama creation, image stitching, and so on. These apps compute orientation from common pixels across image samples and align the images in one target orientation. The resulting image looks as if it has been stitched by joining the end of one image to another.
- **Satellites or space vehicles**: In the remote operation of satellites or robots, it is hard and erroneous to obtain orientation after a significant motion. If the robot moves along a path on the moon, it might get lost due to an error in its local GPS systems or inertial measurement units. In order to build more robust systems, an image-based orientation of the camera is also computed and fused other sensor data to obtain more robust motion estimates.

- **Augmented Reality**: With the boom in smartphones and apps and the availability of better hardware, several computer vision algorithms that use geometry information can now run in real time. **Augmented Reality (AR)** apps and games use geometrical properties from a sequence of images. These further combine this information with other sensor data to create a seamless AR experience and we can see a virtual object as if it is a real object placed on the table. Tracking planar objects and computing the relative positions of objects and the camera is crucial in these applications.

Image formation

The basic camera model is a pinhole camera, though the real-world cameras that we use are far more complex models. A pinhole camera is made up of a very small slit on a plane that allows the formation of an image as depicted in the following figure:

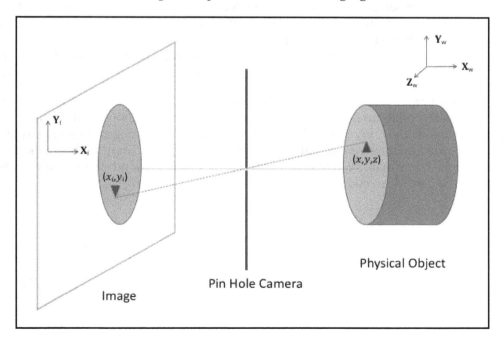

This camera converts a point in the physical world, often termed the *real world*, to a pixel on an image plane. The conversion follows the transformation of the three-dimensional coordinate to two-dimensional coordinates. Here in the image plane, the coordinates are denoted as where $P_i = (x_i, y_i)$, P_i is any point on an image. In the physical world, the same point is denoted by $P_w = (x, y, x)$, where P_w is any point in the physical world with a global reference frame.

$P_i(x', y')$ and $P_w(x, y, z)$ can be related as, for an ideal pin hole camera:

$$x' = f\frac{x}{z}$$
$$y' = f\frac{y}{z}$$

Here, *f* is focal length of the camera.

For further discussion on geometry of image formation, it is necessary to introduce the homogeneous coordinate system. The physical world coordinate system is referred to as **Euclidean coordinate system**. In the image plane, a point *P'* with *(x, y)* coordinates is represented in homogeneous coordinate system as *(x, y, 1)*. Similarly a point P_w with *(x, y, z)* in world coordinates can be represented in homogeneous coordinate system as (x, y, z, 1) .

To convert back from homogeneous to Euclidean, we need to divide by the last coordinate value. To convert a point on an image plane in homogeneous system as (x,y, w) to Euclidean system as (x/w, y/w) . Similarly, for a 3D point in a homogeneous system given by (x, y, z, w), the Euclidean coordinates are given by (x/w, y/w, z/ w). In this book, the use of homogeneous coordinate systems will be explicitly mentioned; otherwise we will see equations in the Euclidean coordinate system.

Image formation comes from transforming physical world coordinates to image plane coordinates but losing information about an extra dimension. This means that when we construct an image we are losing depth information for each pixel. As a result, converting back from image pixel coordinates to real-world coordinates is not possible. As shown in the following figure, for a point P_I in the figure there can be an infinite number of points lying along the line. Points **P1**, **P2**, and **P3** have the same image pixel location, and therefore estimations of depth (distance from camera) are lost during image formation:

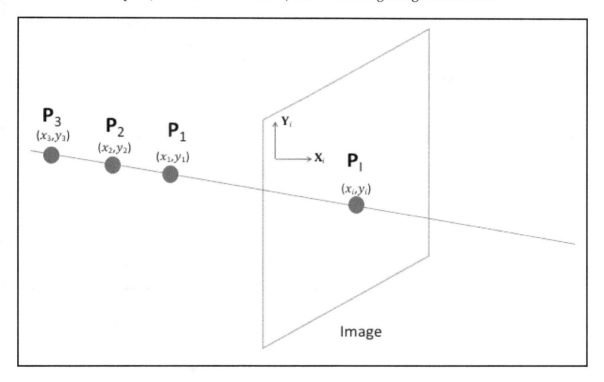

Let us observe a point world from two images. If we know the optical center of a camera that constructs an image and the point location of two images, we can get much more information. The following figure explains **Epipolar Geometry** using two images:

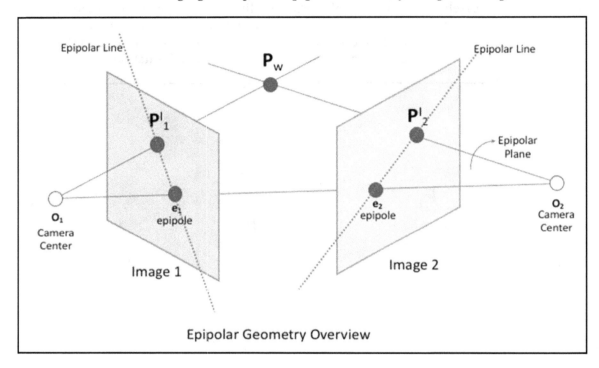

Epipolar Geometry Overview

In the previous figure, the camera centers $\mathbf{O_1}$ and $\mathbf{O_2}$ are connected to point $\mathbf{P_w}$ in the world, and the plane forming the line $\mathbf{P_w}$, $\mathbf{O_1}$, $\mathbf{O_2}$ is the epipolar plane. The points where the camera's center line O_1O_2 intersects with the image are epipoles for the image. These may or may not lie on the image. In cases where both the image planes are parallel, the epipoles will lie at infinity. Here, we can define an epipolar constraint, as if we know the transformation between camera center $\mathbf{O_1}$ and $\mathbf{O_2}$ as translation T and rotation R, we can compute the location of point **P1** in **Image 1** to the corresponding location in **Image 2**. Mathematically, this is written as follows:

$$p_{I_1}^T \cdot [T \times (Rp_{I_2})] = 0$$

Inversely, if know the location of corresponding points in two images, we would like to compute the rotation matrix R and translation matrix T between the two camera centers. Here, if the two cameras are different, the camera centers can be at the different distance from the image plane and, therefore, we would require camera intrinsic parameters too. Mathematically, this is written as follows:

$$p_{I_1}^T \cdot F \cdot p_{I_2} = 0 \text{ where } F = K_1^{-T} \cdot [T_\times] \cdot RK_2^{-1}$$

Here, F is called the **fundamental matrix** and K is our **camera intrinsic matrix** for each camera. Computing F, we can know the correct transformation between the two camera poses and can convert any point on one image plane to another.

In the next section, we will see transformations between images and their applications.

Aligning images

Image alignment is a problem for computing a transformation matrix so that on applying that transformation to an input image, it can be converted to the target image plane. As a result, the resulting images look like they are stitched together and form a continuous larger image.

Panorama is one such example of aligning images, where we collect images of a scene with changing camera angles and the resulting image is a combination of images aligned. A resulting image is as shown, as follows:

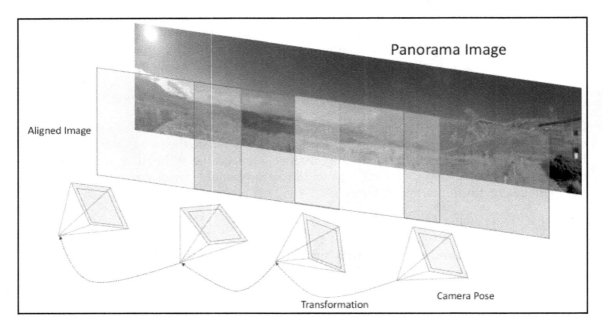

In the preceding figure, an example of panorama creation is shown. Using a camera, we collect multiple images for the same scene by adding overlapping regions. As the camera is moved, often, the pose changes significantly, so therefore for different poses of the camera a transformation matrix is computed.

Let's get started with a basic method to compute this transformation matrix. The following code works inside Jupyter notebook too. In the following block of code, we define a function to compute **oriented BRIEF (ORB)** keypoints. There is a descriptor for each keypoint also:

```
import numpy as np
import matplotlib.pyplot as plt
import cv2
print(cv2.__version__)
import glob
# With jupyter notebook uncomment below line
# %matplotlib inline
# This plots figures inside the notebook
```

```
def compute_orb_keypoints(filename):
    """
    Reads image from filename and computes ORB keypoints
    Returns image, keypoints and descriptors.
    """
    # load image
    img = cv2.imread(filename)
    # create orb object
    orb = cv2.ORB_create()
    # set method for extraction orb points
    orb.setScoreType(cv2.FAST_FEATURE_DETECTOR_TYPE_9_16)
    orb.setWTA_K(3)
    # detect keypoints
    kp = orb.detect(img,None)

    # for detected keypoints compute descriptors.
    kp, des = orb.compute(img, kp)
    return img,kp, des
```

Once we have feature keypoints, we match them using a brute force matcher, as follows:

```
def brute_force_matcher(des1, des2):
    """
    Brute force matcher to match ORB feature descriptors
    """
    # create BFMatcher object
    bf = cv2.BFMatcher(cv2.NORM_HAMMING2, crossCheck=True)
    # Match descriptors.
    matches = bf.match(des1,des2)

    # Sort them in the order of their distance.
    matches = sorted(matches, key = lambda x:x.distance)

    return matches
```

This is our main function for computing the fundamental matrix:

```python
def compute_fundamental_matrix(filename1, filename2):
    """
    Takes in filenames of two input images
    Return Fundamental matrix computes
    using 8 point algorithm
    """
    # compute ORB keypoints and descriptor for each image
    img1, kp1, des1 = compute_orb_keypoints(filename1)
    img2, kp2, des2 = compute_orb_keypoints(filename2)
    # compute keypoint matches using descriptor
    matches = brute_force_matcher(des1, des2)
    # extract points
    pts1 = []
    pts2 = []
    for i,(m) in enumerate(matches):
        if m.distance < 20:
            #print(m.distance)
            pts2.append(kp2[m.trainIdx].pt)
            pts1.append(kp1[m.queryIdx].pt)
    pts1 = np.asarray(pts1)
    pts2 = np.asarray(pts2)
    # Compute fundamental matrix
    F, mask = cv2.findFundamentalMat(pts1,pts2,cv2.FM_8POINT)
    return F



# read list of images form dir in sorted order
# change here to path to dataset
image_dir = '/Users/mac/Documents/dinoRing/'
file_list = sorted(glob.glob(image_dir+'*.png'))

#compute F matrix between two images
print(compute_fundamental_matrix(file_list[0], file_list[2]))
```

In the next section, we will extend relative transformation between images to compute camera pose and also estimate the trajectory of the camera.

Visual odometry

Odometry is the process of incrementally estimating the position of a robot or device. In the case of a wheeled robot, it uses wheel motion or inertial measurement using tools such as gyroscopes or accelerometers to estimate the robot's position by summing over wheel rotations. Using **visual odometry (VO)**, we can estimate the odometry of cameras using only image sequences by continuously estimating camera motion.

A major use of VO is in autonomous robots like drones, where gyroscopes and accelerometers are not robust enough for motion estimation. However, there are several assumptions and challenges in using VO:

- Firstly, objects in the scene for the camera should be static. While the camera captures a sequence of the image, the only moving object should be the camera itself.
- Moreover, during the estimation of VO, if there are significant illumination changes, like light source appearance, drastic changes to pixel values might occur in subsequent images. As a result, VO suffers from large errors or complete dysfunction. The same case applies to dark environments; due to the lack of illumination, VO is not able to estimate robust motion.

The process of VO is described as follows:

1. Initialize the starting position as the origin, for the frame of reference. All the subsequent motion estimation is done with respect to this frame.
2. As an image arrives, compute features and match corresponding features with previous frames to get a transformation matrix.
3. Use the historical transformation matrix between all subsequent frames to compute the trajectory of the camera.

This process is shown in the following figure:

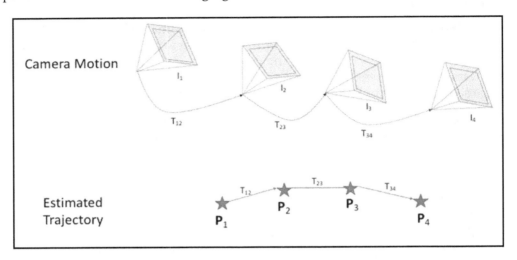

Here, I_i is the ith image received from the camera and T_{ij} is the transformation matrix computed using feature matching between i and j images. The trajectory of camera motion is shown with stars, where P_i is the estimated pose of the camera at the ith image. This can be a two-dimensional pose with (x, y) angle as well as a three-dimensional pose. Each P_j is computed as applying the transformation T_{ij} on P_i.

Other than the assumption mentioned earlier, there are a few limitations to VO estimation:

- As more images are observed from the sequence, the errors in trajectory estimation are accumulated. This results in an overall drift in the computed track of camera motion.
- In cases of sudden motion in camera, the image feature match between the corresponding two images will be significantly erroneous. As a result, the estimated transformation between the frames will also have huge errors and, therefore, the overall trajectory of camera motion gets highly distorted.

Visual SLAM

SLAM refers to Simultaneous Localization and Mapping and is one of the most common problems in robot navigation. Since a mobile robot does not have hardcoded information about the environment around itself, it uses sensors onboard to construct a representation of the region. The robot tries to estimate its position with respect to objects around it like trees, building, and so on. This is, therefore, a chicken-egg problem, where the robot first tries to localize itself using objects around it and then uses its obtained location to map objects around it; hence the term *Simultaneous Localization and Mapping*. There are several methods for solving the SLAM problem. In this section, we will discuss special types of SLAM using a single RGB camera.

Visual SLAM methods extend visual odometry by computing a more robust camera trajectory as well as constructing a robust representation of the environment. An overview of Visual SLAM in action is shown in the following figure:

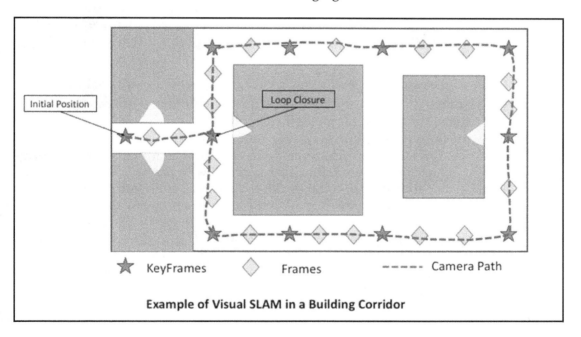

Example of Visual SLAM in a Building Corridor

This is an overview of a generic SLAM method composed of an undirected graph. Each node of the graph is composed of a keyframe which represents unique information about the world and also contains the camera pose (x,y, angle) for the location. In between, keyframes are frames that overlap significantly with the keyframes scene, however, they help in computing robust estimates of pose for the next frame. Here, a camera starts the process by initializing a keyframe at the origin. As the camera moves along a trajectory, the SLAM system updates the graph by adding keyframes or frames based on criteria. If the camera returns back to a previously seen area, it links up with the old frame, creating a cyclic structure in the graph. This is often called **loop closure** and helps correct the overall graph structure. The edges connecting nodes to another in the graph are usually weighted with a transformation matrix between the pose of the two nodes. Overall, the graph structure is corrected by improving the position of keyframes. This is done by minimizing overall error. Once a graph is constructed, it can be saved and used for localizing a camera by matching to the nearest keyframe.

In this section, we will see a popular robust method, ORB SLAM, using monocular cameras. This method constructs a graph structure similar to that which was shown previously to keep track of camera pose and works on RGB image frames from a simple camera. The steps involved can be summarized as:

1. **Input**: In the case of the monocular camera, the input is a single captured frame.
2. **Initialization**: Once the process starts, a map is initialized with the origin, and the first node of a keyframe graph is constructed.
3. There are three threads that run in parallel for the system:
    - **Tracking**: For each incoming frame, ORB features are extracted for matching. These features are matched with previously seen frames and are then used to compute the relative pose of the current frame. This also decides if the current frame is to be kept as a keyframe or used as a normal frame.
    - **Local mapping**: If a new keyframe is determined from tracking, the overall map is updated with the insertion of a new node in the graph. While a new connection between neighbourhood keyframes is formed, redundant connections are removed.

- **Loop closure**: If there is a previously seen keyframe that matches the current keyframe, a loop is formed. This gives extra information about drift caused by the trajectory of the camera pose and as a result, all node poses in the graph map is corrected by an optimization algorithm.

In the following section, we will use an implementation of ORB SLAM2 from `https://github.com/raulmur/ORB_SLAM2`. This is not a Python-based implementation. The instruction provided there can be used to build the package and can be used to see visual SLAM. However, for demonstration purposes, we will use a Docker container version of it.

A Docker is a container platform that provides the distributed shipping of an environment as if they are packed inside a ship container, as well as code to run applications. We need to install the Docker platform and pull an image of the environment, as well as the code. The environment inside the image is independent of the platform we use, as long as the Docker platform is installed. If you want to learn more about Docker and containers, the following website provides more details, as well as installation instructions: `https://www.docker.com/what-docker`.

Once Docker is installed, we can begin with the following steps for ORB SLAM 2. Let's start by pulling a Docker image (this is similar to cloning a repository) for ORB SLAM:

```
docker pull resbyte/orb-slam2
```

This will download the environment for the package and pre-build the ORB SLAM2 repository so that we don't have to build it again. All the dependencies for this repository are already satisfied inside the Docker image.

Once the Docker image is downloaded, let's get started with downloading the dataset. In this section, we will use the `TUM RGBD` dataset, which was collected specifically to evaluate SLAM and VO methods. Earlier in this chapter, under dataset and libraries, we saw how to download this dataset. We will use the extracted dataset in the following section.

Since this implementation of ORB SLAM uses a GUI interface to output the results, we will first add the GUI interface to the Docker image. The following code assumes a Linux environment.

For the GUI output from ORB SLAM, add this as the first step, otherwise, visual SLAM will run but there will be an error:

```
xhost +local:docker
```

Now, let's launch the downloaded image using the Docker platform, though with several parameters:

```
docker run -ti --rm   -e DISPLAY=$DISPLAY   -v /tmp/.X11-unix:/tmp/.X11-
unix   -v /home/rgbd_dataset_freiburg1_xyz:/root/rgbd_dataset_freiburg1_xyz
orb-slam:latest /bin/bash
```

Here, the -e and -v parameters are used to set the display environment for GUI. The dataset downloaded before is shared inside Docker using -v $PATH_TO_DOWNLOADED_DATASET:$PATH_INSIDE_DOCKER. Finally, the name of the image is `orb-slam: latest`, which we downloaded earlier using Docker pull, and we asked it to run bash inside Docker using `/bin/bash`.

On running the previous command, we can see a change in the Terminal, as if we logging in to a new computer Terminal. Let's go and run ORB-SLAM as follows:

```
cd ORB_SLAM2

# run orb slam
./Examples/Monocular/mono_tum Vocabulary/ORBvoc.txt
Examples/Monocular/TUM1.yaml /root/rgbd_dataset_freiburg1_xyz
```

Here, the first parameter is to run Monocular Visual SLAM, as there are other methods too. The other parameters are to run the type of dataset that we had downloaded earlier. If there is any change in the dataset, these parameters are to be changed accordingly.

On this command, after some time there will be two windows, shown as follows:

Here, the window on the right is the input dataset, with the keypoints detected in each frame. While the window on the left details the Visual SLAM happening. As we can see there are blue boxes that show the keyframe graph creation, with the current state of the position of the camera and its links with the historical position. As the camera in the dataset is moved, the graph is created and adjusted as more observations are found. The result is an accurate trajectory of the camera as well as adjusted keypoints.

Summary

In this chapter, the aim was to view computer vision from a geometrical point of view. Starting with understanding how an image is formed using a pinhole camera, there was a discussion on how to incorporate three-dimensional worlds using multi-image formation. We saw an explanation of Visual Odometry with an introduction to Visual SLAM. The various steps involved in SLAM were explained and a demo of using ORB-SLAM was also shown, so that we could see a SLAM operation as it happened. This is basic motivation to extend the SLAM solution for various other datasets, and so create interesting applications.

References

- Sturm Jürgen, Nikolas Engelhard, Felix Endres, Wolfram Burgard, and Daniel Cremers. *A Benchmark for the Evaluation of RGB-D SLAM Systems*. In Intelligent Robots and Systems (IROS), 2012 IEEE/RSJ International Conference on, pp. 573-580. IEEE, 2012.
- Mur-Artal Raul, Jose Maria Martinez Montiel, and Juan D. Tardos. *ORB-SLAM: A Versatile and Accurate Monocular SLAM System*. IEEE Transactions on Robotics 31, no. 5 (2015): 1147-1163.
- Rublee Ethan, Vincent Rabaud, Kurt Konolige, and Gary Bradski. *ORB: an efficient alternative to SIFT or SURF*. In Computer Vision (ICCV), 2011 IEEE international conference on, pp. 2564-2571. IEEE, 2011.

A
Mathematics for Computer Vision

In the book, we are using several advanced algorithms that require a good background in mathematics. This appendix begins by describing some prerequisites, with Python implementations wherever required.

In this appendix, we will cover the following topics:

- Linear algebraic operation and properties of vectors and matrices
- Probability and common probabilistic functions

Datasets and libraries

In this appendix, we won't use a specific dataset; rather, we will use example values to show the workings. The libraries used are NumPy and scipy. In Chapter 2, *Libraries, Development Platform, and Datasets* we saw the installation of the Anaconda tool, which has both NumPy and SciPy; therefore, there is no need of a new installation.

If Anaconda is not installed, then to install Numpy and SciPy, use the following command:

```
pip install numpy scipy
```

To plot a figure, we will use matplotlib. This also comes with Anaconda; however, if there is a need for installation, use the following command:

```
pip install matplotlib
```

To begin with the codes in the chapter, we will use this common import:

```
import numpy as np
import scipy
import matplotlib.pyplot as plt
```

Linear algebra

Computer vision tools and techniques are highly dependent on linear algebraic operations. We will use see an explanation of basic to advanced operations that are required in developing CV applications.

Vectors

In a 2D plane, vectors are denoted as a point $p = (x, y)$.

In this case, the magnitude of p is denoted as $||p||$ and is given by the following:

$$||p|| = \sqrt{x^2 + y^2}$$

In Python, a vector is denoted by a one-dimensional array, as follows:

```
p = [1, 2, 3]
```

Here, the common properties required are length of the vector and magnitude of the vector, which is given as follows:

```
print(len(p))
```

```
>>> 3
```

Common vector operations are as follows:

- Addition
- Subtraction
- Vector multiplication
- Vector norm
- Orthogonality

Addition

Let's say there are two vectors denoted as follows:

```
v1 = np.array([2, 3, 4, 5])
v2 = np.array([4, 5, 6, 7])
```

The resulting vector is the element-wise sum, as follows:

```
print(v1 + v2)

>>> array([ 6, 8, 10, 12])
```

Subtraction

Subtraction is similar to addition; instead of the element-wise sum, we compute the element-wise difference:

```
v1 = np.array([2, 3, 4, 5])
v2 = np.array([4, 5, 6, 7])
print(v1 - v2)

>>> array([-2, -2, -2, -2])
```

Vector multiplication

There are two methods of computing vector multiplication:

- Inner product—this is also known as dot product and is the sum of element-wise products of two vectors:

$$inner(V_1, V_2) = \sum_i v_1^i \times v_2^i$$

Where v_i^i and v_2^i are ith elements of vectors V_1 and V_2 respectively.

In Python, we can compute this using NumPy:

```
v1 = np.array([2, 3, 4, 5])
v2 = np.array([4, 5, 6, 7])
print(np.inner(v1, v2))

>>> 82
```

- Outer product—this takes in two vectors and computes a matrix

$V_3 = V_1 \times V_2$ where each element i, j in V_3 is given as:

$$v_3(i, j) = v_1^i \times v_2^j$$

In Python we can compute this as follows:

```
v1 = np.array([2, 3, 4, 5])
v2 = np.array([4, 5, 6, 7])
print(np.outer(v1, v2))

>>> array([[ 8, 10, 12, 14],
[12, 15, 18, 21],
[16, 20, 24, 28],
[20, 25, 30, 35]])
```

Vector norm

A l_pth order norm of a vector V is given as follows:

$$||V||_p = (\sum_i^n |v_i|^p)^{1/p}$$

There are two popular kinds of norms for vectors:

- l_1 norm—this is given as $||V||_1 = \sum_i |v_i|$ and an example is as shown here:

```
v = np.array([2, 3, 4, 5])
print(np.linalg.norm(v, ord=1))

>>>14.0
```

- l_2 norm—this is given as $||V||_2 = (\sum_i |v_i|^2)^{1/2}$ and an example is as follows:

```
v = np.array([2, 3, 4, 5])
print(np.linalg.norm(v, ord=2))

>>>7.34846922835
```

Orthogonality

Two vectors are said to be orthogonal if their inner product is zero. From the geometric point of view, if the two vectors are perpendicular, they are said to be orthogonal to each other:

```
v1 = np.array([2, 3, 4, 5])
v2 = np.array([1,-1,-1,1]) # orthogonal to v1
np.inner(v1, v2)

>>> 0
```

Matrices

Two-dimensional arrays are referred to as matrices and, in computer vision, these play a significant role. An image in the digital world is represented as a matrix; hence, the operations that we will study here are applicable to images as well.

Matrix A is denoted as follows:

$$
A = \begin{bmatrix}
a_{11} & a_{12} & \cdots & a_{1n} \\
a_{21} & a_{22} & \cdots & a_{2n} \\
\vdots & \vdots & \vdots & \vdots \\
a_{m1} & a_{m2} & \cdots & a_{mn}
\end{bmatrix}
$$

Here, the shape of the matrix is m x n with m rows and n columns. If $m = n$, the matrix is termed as a square matrix.

In Python, we can make a sample matrix, as follows:

```
A = np.array([[1, 2, 3],[4, 5, 6], [7, 8, 9]])
```

This is printed as follows:

```
print(A)

>>> array([[1, 2, 3],
[4, 5, 6],
[7, 8, 9]])
```

Operations on matrices

We will be performing similar operations on matrices as we did on vectors. The only difference will be in the way we perform these operations. To understand this in detail, go through the following sections.

Addition

In order to perform the addition of two matrices A and B, both of them should be of the same shape. The addition operation is an element-wise addition done to create a matrix C of the same shape as A and B. Here is an example:

```
A = np.array([[1, 2, 3],[4, 5, 6], [7, 8, 9]])
B = np.array([[1,1,1], [1,1,1], [1,1,1]])
C = A+B
print(C)

>>> array([[ 2, 3, 4],
 [ 5, 6, 7],
 [ 8, 9, 10]])
```

Subtraction

Similar to addition, subtracting matrix B from matrix A requires both of them to be of the same shape. The resulting matrix C will be of the same shape as A and B. The following is an example of subtracting B from A:

```
A = np.array([[1, 2, 3],[4, 5, 6], [7, 8, 9]])
B = np.array([[1,1,1], [1,1,1], [1,1,1]])
C = A - B
print(C)

>>> array([[0, 1, 2],
 [3, 4, 5],
 [6, 7, 8]])
```

Matrix multiplication

Let there be two matrices: A with size $m \times n$ and B with size $q \times p$. The assumption here is that $n == q$. Now, the two matrices of sizes $m \times n$ and $n \times p$ are compatible for matrix multiplication. The multiplication is given as follows:

$$C = AB$$

Here, each element in C is given as follows:

$$c_{i,j} = \sum_{k=1}^{n} a_{i,k} b_{k,j}$$

This is performed with Python, as follows:

```
# A matrix of size (2x3)
A = np.array([[1, 2, 3],[4, 5, 6]])
# B matrix of size (3x2)
B = np.array([[1, 0], [0, 1], [1, 0]])
C = np.dot(A, B) # size (2x2)
print(C)

>>> array([[ 4, 2],
[10, 5]])
```

Since matrix multiplication depends on the order of multiplication, reversing the order may result in a different matrix or an invalid multiplication due to size mismatch.

We have seen the basic operations with matrices; now we will some properties of them.

Matrix properties

There are a few properties that are used on matrices for executing mathematical operations. They are mentioned in detail in this section.

Transpose

When we interchange columns and rows of a matrix with each other, the resulting matrix is termed as the transpose of the matrix and is denoted as A^T, for an original matrix A. An example of this is as follows:

```
A = np.array([[1, 2, 3],[4, 5, 6]])
np.transpose(A)

>>> array([[1, 4],
[2, 5],
[3, 6]])
```

Identity matrix

This is a special kind of matrix with diagonal elements as 1 and all other elements as zero:

```
I = np.identity(3) # size of identity matrix
print(I)

>>> [[ 1.  0.  0.]
 [ 0.  1.  0.]
 [ 0.  0.  1.]]
```

An interesting property of the identity matrix is that it doesn't modify target matrix after multiplication, that is $C = AI$ or $C = IA$ will result in $C = I$.

Diagonal matrix

Extending the definition of an identity matrix, in a diagonal matrix, the entries of a matrix along the main diagonal are non-zero and the rest of the values are zero. An example is as follows:

```
A = np.array([[12,0,0],[0,50,0],[0,0,43]])

>>> array([[12,  0,  0],
 [ 0, 50,  0],
 [ 0,  0, 43]])
```

Symmetric matrix

In a symmetric matrix, the elements follow a property: $a_{i,j} = a_{j,i}$. This element wise property for a given symmetric matrix A, can also be defined in terms of a transpose as $A^T = A$.

Let's consider an asymmetric square matrix (with size $n \times n$) given as follows:

```
A = np.array([[1, 2, 3],[4, 5, 6], [7, 8, 9]])
```

Its transpose can be computed, as follows:

```
A_T = np.transpose(A)

>>> [[1 4 7]
 [2 5 8]
 [3 6 9]]
```

We can show that $A + A^T$ is a symmetric matrix:

```
print(A + A_T)

>>> [[ 2 6 10]
 [ 6 10 14]
 [10 14 18]]
```

Here, we can see that the elements $a_{i,j} = a_{j,i}$.

Also, we can compute anti-symmetric matrix as $A - A^T$, where each element $a_{i,j} = -a_{j,i}$:

```
print(A - A_T)

>>> [[ 0 -2 -4]
 [ 2  0 -2]
 [ 4  2  0]]
```

An important property arises from this; we can break any square matrix into a summation of symmetric and anti-symmetric matrix, as follows:

$$A = 0.5 * (A + A_T) + 0.5 * (A - A_T)$$

Continuing the Python Scripts as follows:

```
symm = A + A_T
anti_symm = A - A_T
print(0.5*symm + 0.5*anti_symm)

>>> [[ 1. 2. 3.]
 [ 4. 5. 6.]

 [ 7. 8. 9.]]
```

Trace of a matrix

The trace of a matrix is the sum of all its diagonal elements:

```
A = np.array([[1, 2, 3],[4, 5, 6], [7, 8, 9]])

np.trace(A)
```

Determinant

Geometrically, the absolute value of a determinant of a matrix is the volume enclosed by taking each row as a vector. This can be computed, as follows:

```
A = np.array([[2, 3],[ 5, 6]])
print(np.linalg.det(A))

>>> -2.9999999999999982
```

Norm of a matrix

Continuing the norm formulation from the previous section on vectors, in a matrix, the most common type of norm is the Frobenius norm:

$$||A|| = \sqrt{\left(\sum_i \sum_j a_{i,j}^2\right)} = \sqrt{tr(A^T A)}$$

In Python we compute this as follows:

```
A = np.array([[1, 2, 3],[4, 5, 6], [7, 8, 9]])
np.linalg.norm(A)

>>> 16.881943016134134
```

Getting the inverse of a matrix

An inverse of a matrix, denoted as A^{-1}, has an interesting property; $AA^{-1} = I = A^{-1}A$. The inverse is unique for each matrix; however, not all matrices have inverse matrices. An example of inverse of matrix is as follows:

```
A = np.array([[1, 2, 3],[5, 4, 6], [9, 8, 7]])
A_inv = np.linalg.inv(A)
print(A_inv)

>>>[[ -6.66666667e-01 3.33333333e-01 4.93432455e-17]
 [ 6.33333333e-01 -6.66666667e-01 3.00000000e-01]
 [ 1.33333333e-01 3.33333333e-01 -2.00000000e-01]]
```

Now, if we take a product of A and A^{-1}, we get the following result:

```
np.dot(A, A_inv)

>>> [[ 1.00000000e+00  1.66533454e-16 -5.55111512e-17]
 [ 3.33066907e-16  1.00000000e+00  1.11022302e-16]
 [ 8.32667268e-16 -2.77555756e-16  1.00000000e+00]]
```

We can see that the diagonal elements are 1 and all others are approximately 0.

Orthogonality

Another property associated with a square matrix is orthogonality, where $A^T A = I$ or $AA^T = I$. This is also leads to $A^T = A^{-1}$.

Computing eigen values and eigen vectors

The eigenvalue λ of a square matrix A has the property such that any transformation on it with eigen vector x is equal to the scalar multiplication of λ with A:

$$Ax = \lambda x \text{ where } x \neq 0$$

To compute eigenvalues and eigen vectors of A, we need to solve the characteristic equation, as follows:

$$|\lambda I - A| = 0$$

Here, I is an identity matrix of the same size as A:

We can do this using NumPy as follows:

```
A = np.array([[1, 2, 3],[5, 4, 6], [9, 8, 7]])
eigvals, eigvectors = np.linalg.eig(A)
print("Eigen Values: ", eigvals)
print("Eigen Vectors:", eigvectors)

>>> Eigen Values: [ 15.16397149 -2.30607508 -0.85789641]
Eigen Vectors: [[-0.24668682 -0.50330679 0.54359359]
[-0.5421775 -0.3518559 -0.8137192 ]
[-0.80323668 0.78922728 0.20583261]]
```

Hessian matrix

A first-order gradient matrix of A is formed by computing partial gradients on each element of A:

$$\nabla_A f(A) = \begin{bmatrix} \dfrac{\partial f(A)}{\partial a_{11}} & \dfrac{\partial f(A)}{\partial a_{12}} & \cdots & \dfrac{\partial f(A)}{\partial a_{1n}} \\[2ex] \dfrac{\partial f(A)}{\partial a_{21}} & \dfrac{\partial f(A)}{\partial a_{22}} & \cdots & \dfrac{\partial f(A)}{\partial a_{2n}} \\[2ex] \vdots & \vdots & \vdots & \vdots \\[2ex] \dfrac{\partial f(A)}{\partial a_{m1}} & \dfrac{\partial f(A)}{\partial a_{m2}} & \cdots & \dfrac{\partial f(A)}{\partial a_{mn}} \end{bmatrix}$$

Similarly, the second-order gradient of A for a function f is given as follows:

$$\nabla_A^2 f(A) = \begin{bmatrix} \dfrac{\partial^2 f(A)}{\partial a_{11}^2} & \dfrac{\partial^2 f(A)}{\partial a_{12}^2} & \cdots & \dfrac{\partial^2 f(A)}{\partial a_{1n}^2} \\[2ex] \dfrac{\partial^2 f(A)}{\partial a_{21}^2} & \dfrac{\partial^2 f(A)}{\partial a_{22}^2} & \cdots & \dfrac{\partial^2 f(A)}{\partial a_{2n}^2} \\[2ex] \vdots & \vdots & \vdots & \vdots \\[2ex] \dfrac{\partial^2 f(A)}{\partial a_{m1}^2} & \dfrac{\partial^2 f(A)}{\partial a_{m2}^2} & \cdots & \dfrac{\partial^2 f(A)}{\partial a_{mn}^2} \end{bmatrix}$$

The Hessian is denoted by $\det(\nabla_A^2 f(A))$.

Singular Value Decomposition

Singular Value Decomposition (SVD) is used to perform decomposition of a matrix A into $U\Sigma V^{-1}$, where U and V^{-1} are orthogonal matrices and Σ is a diagonal matrix:

```
A = np.array([[1, 2, 3],[5, 4, 6], [9, 8, 7]])

U, s, V = np.linalg.svd(A, full_matrices=True)
```

Introduction to probability theory

We have studied probability in several courses through university or elsewhere. In this section, the aim is to fill in the gaps, so that computer vision algorithms that require probability theory can be easily built upon. The motivation to use probability theory in computer vision is to model uncertainty.

What are random variables?

Random variables are used to define the possibilities of an event in terms of real numbers. The values it can represent are random and, by applying certain assumptions, we can restrict it to given range. To get started with random variables, we need to either compute a function that approximates its behavior or assume and prove our hypothesis function through experimentation. These functions are of two types:

- In the discrete domain, random variables' values are discrete. Then the function used to model probabilities is termed as **Probability Mass Function (PMF)**. For example, let x be a discrete random variable; its PMF is given by $P(x = k)$, where k is one of the K different values of random variable x.
- In the continuous domain, the function to model random variable's is termed as **Probability Density Function (PDF)**, which takes in continuous domain values of a random variable x to produce probabilities $p(x)$.

Expectation

For a discrete random variable x, the expectation of a function f is given as follows:

$$\mathbb{E}_{x \sim P}[f(x)] = \sum_x P(x)f(x)$$

Here $P(x)$ is the probability mass function.

For a continuous random variable x, the expectation of a function f is given as follows:

$$\mathbb{E}_{x \sim p}[f(x)] = \int p(x)f(x)dx$$

Variance

To measure the quality of concentration of a random variable x, we use variance. Mathematically, it is defined as follows:

$$Var[x] = \mathbb{E}[(x - \mathbb{E}(x))^2]$$

This expression can also be converted into:

$$Var[x] = \mathbb{E}[x^2] - \mathbb{E}[x]^2$$

Probability distributions

The distributions are explained in detail in the following sections.

Bernoulli distribution

In Bernoulli distribution the function is given as follows:

$$p(x) = \begin{cases} p & \text{if } k = 1 \\ 1 - p & \text{if } k = 0 \end{cases}$$

Here, the parameter is p and we can model this using SciPy as:

```
from scipy.stats import bernoulli
import matplotlib.pyplot as plt

# parameters for bernoulli distribution
p = 0.3
# create random variable
random_variable = bernoulli( p)
```

Binomial distribution

In Binomial distribution the function is given as $p(x) = \binom{n}{x}p^x(1-p)^{n-x}$, with parameters n and p. We can model this using SciPy:

```
from scipy.stats import binom
import matplotlib.pyplot as plt

# parameters for binomial distribution
```

```
n = 10
p = 0.3

# create random variable
random_variable = binom(n, p)

# compute probability mass function
x = scipy.linspace(0,10,11)

# plot
plt.figure(figsize=(12, 8))
plt.vlines(x, 0, random_variable.pmf(x))
plt.show()
```

The resulting plot can be seen as follows:

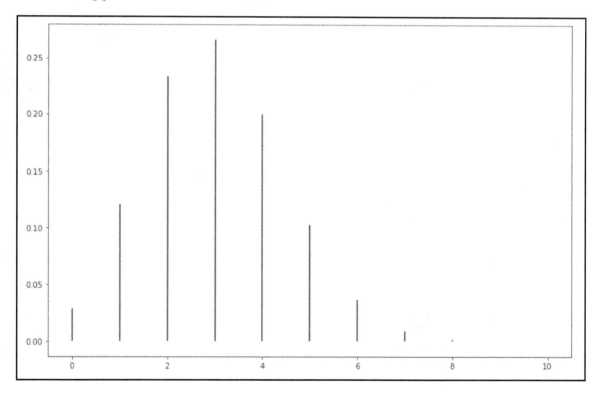

Poisson distribution

The function for Poisson distribution is as follows:

$$p(x) = \exp(-\lambda)\frac{\lambda^x}{x!}$$

Here, the parameter is λ and an example script in SciPy is as follows:

```
from scipy.stats import poisson
import matplotlib.pyplot as plt

# parameters for bernoulli distribution
lambda_ = 0.1

# create random variable
random_variable = poisson(lambda_)

# compute probability mass function
x = scipy.linspace(0,5,11)

# plot
plt.figure(figsize=(12, 8))
plt.vlines(x, 0, random_variable.pmf(x))
plt.show()
```

Uniform distribution

A distribution between a and b is said to be uniform if it follows this:

$$p(x) = \begin{cases} \frac{1}{b-a} & \text{if } a \leq x \leq b \\ 0 & \text{otherwise} \end{cases}$$

Gaussian distribution

One of the most common distributions used in computer vision, Gaussian distribution is defined as follows:

$$p(x) = \frac{1}{\sqrt{2\pi}\sigma}\exp(-\frac{(x-\mu)^2}{2\sigma^2})$$

Here, the parameters are μ and σ, which are also termed as **mean** and **variance**. A special case arises when μ is 0 and σ is 1.0; it is termed as normal distribution. Using SciPy, we can model it as follows:

```
from scipy.stats import norm
import matplotlib.pyplot as plt
import scipy

# create random variable
random_variable = norm()

# compute probability mass function
x = scipy.linspace(-5,5,20)

# plot
plt.figure(figsize=(12, 8))
plt.vlines(x, 0, random_variable.pdf(x))
plt.show()
```

The resulting plot can be seen as follows:

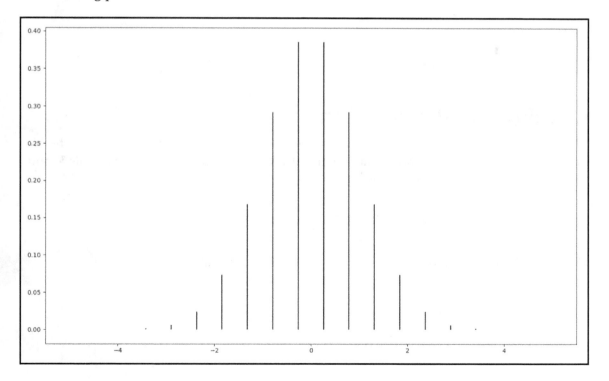

Joint distribution

Joint distribution is used for two random variables, if we would like to find the effective probabilities if the two events associated with them happen together. Let x and y be the two random variables; their joint distribution function is given by $P(x, y)$.

Marginal distribution

In the case of joint distribution, we want to know the probability density function of one event assuming we can observe all the other events. We term this marginal distribution and it is given as follows:

$$P_y(y) = \int P(x, y)dx$$

For a discrete case, the marginal distribution is as follows:

$$P_y(y) = \sum_x P(x, y)$$

Here, we are finding the marginal distribution of y with respect to x.

Conditional distribution

We would like to compute the probabilities after having known the values of one of the random variables. This is denoted mathematically as $P_{x|y}(x|y)$ for the known variable y, and a relation with joint probability distribution is given as follows:

$$P_{x|y}(x|y) = \frac{P(x, y)}{P_y(y)}$$

Here, $P(x, y)$ is the joint distribution and $Py(y)$ is the marginal distribution.

Bayes theorem

An important theorem used implicitly in many computer vision applications is Bayes theorem, which extends conditional probabilities as follows in the case of a continuous random variable:

$$P_{x|y}(x|y) = \frac{P(x,y)}{P_y(y)} = \frac{P_{y|x}(y|x)P_x(x)}{P_y(y)}$$

Here, we have:

$$P_y(y) = \int_{-\infty}^{\infty} P_{y|x}(y|x')P_x(x')dx'$$

Summary

In this appendix, we explained some prerequisites for computer vision algorithms. Linear algebraic expressions explained here are used in geometric modifications of image, such as translation, rotation, and so on.

Probabilistic approaches are used in a range of applications including, but not limited to, object detection, segmentation, and tracking applications. As such, having a good understanding of these prerequisites will make our application implementation faster and more efficient.

B
Machine Learning for Computer Vision

In this chapter, we will get an overview of the relevant machine learning theory and tools that are useful when developing applications such as image classification, object detection, and so on. With widespread communication tools and the wide availability of camera sensors, we are now bombarded with large amounts of image data. Utilizing this data to create computer vision applications requires an understanding of some basic machine learning concepts.

Let's begin by first explaining what machine learning is, and then we will see the different types of algorithms in it.

What is machine learning?

Let's say we have scanned images of several handwritten digits and want to make a piece of software that would recognize handwritten digits from an image scan. For simplicity, let's assume that we have only one digit. The target software that we develop takes in this image and outputs a number corresponding to that image. We can create an algorithm with several checks, such as: if there is a single vertical line, then output it as 1, or if there is an oval shape, then show it as zero. However, this is very naive and is a bad solution because we can have vertical lines for other digits too: 7, 9, and so on. The following figure explains the overall process, taking in one of the samples from the MNIST handwritten digit dataset:

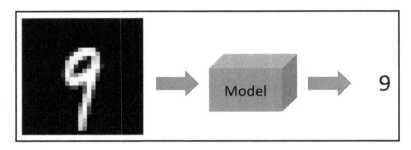

There are several ways to model such a problem. We know that an image is made up of arrays of pixels and each pixel stores a value. In the previous figure, the value of each pixel is binary and an initial approach would be to compute the mean value of the image. Based on this mean value, we can define a function such that if the mean value lies between a range, then the image is of **9**; we can do the same for other digits. In this whole process, our parameters are the ranges for each digit image, and these ranges can be either add intuitively or learned through experience.

However, such a method of detecting digits in an image is prone to errors and is not efficient. The parameters for the model may work only on a specific set of images and it is hard to find the right set of values for the ranges just from experience. The machine learning technique plays an important role here. In this setup, let's use a function that will output an array of size 10, corresponding to the digits we are trying to find. Each array value represents the probability of that digit in the image. The highest probability digit will be the identified digit. Now, we have modeled the output but our input is still the mean value of the image, which may not vary much between different images. So, instead of using the mean value, we can use whole image pixels and map the pixel values directly to the output probabilities. This way, we can capture more variations in the image, and this is the usual way in computer vision.

Our understanding of machine learning can be further strengthened by a mathematical method for modeling the problem, as follows:

$$Y = F_\theta(X)$$

Here, X is the input and Y is the output of the model. In our previous case, these are the images and probability array respectively. F is the machine learning model that we would like to create and θ are the parameters of F.

Kinds of machine learning techniques

In the previous section, we saw an introduction to machine learning and an example modeling of a digit image. Now, we will see the different styles of machine learning techniques.

Supervised learning

In supervised learning, we are given a dataset of both the inputs and required outputs for the model; our goal is to create a model that will take any previously unseen data and output values that are true to the actual as much as possible. There are two kinds of supervised learning.

Classification

This is the term for cases when the output of the model is categorical. For example, in the case of digit classification, the output is one of the 10 different digits.

Regression

This is the term for cases when the output has continuous values, for example, a line fitting model. In it, the goal is to approximate the curve as much as possible so that the output of the model would be a value within a certain range.

Unsupervised learning

In this type of machine learning, we are not given any dataset with specific outputs; instead, the model should be able to find the possible outputs given an input. For example, in the previous handwritten digit image, we would like to estimate all possible digits in some ancient text. The assumption here is that we don't know how many different kinds of digits exist in that text. In such a case, the model should understand what a digit looks like. An example approach could be to segment the regions of the digit in the image and fit approximately basic shapes like lines, circles, rectangles, and so on.

Dimensionality's curse

Given the different kinds of machine learning techniques, it is highly important to know the challenges in modeling. We will use the previous digit classification method. We previously tried to model it using all pixels as the available input. The dimensions for the input are the image size, that is, h x w. It ranges from several hundreds to a few thousand. This size is considered as the input dimension, and as it increases, the computation as well as uncertainty in estimation increase. We need a bigger model to perform better estimation if the input dimension increases. This is termed **curse of dimensionality**.

In order to resolve this curse, it is highly recommended to reduce the input dimensions. For example, instead of using pixel values as input, we can extract strong features and use them as input to the model. This will reduce the input dimensions significantly and may improve the overall performance of the model.

A rolling-ball view of learning

To learn the parameters of the model, we create a `cost` function or `objective` function and minimize its value. The minimum value of `objective` will give the best parameters for the model. For example, let model $F_\theta(X)$ predicts a value Y and also let we are given with the dataset of both the model input and the output. Then, learning a model requires updating the parameters θ such that we get the best performance.

To make the model learn, we use parameter update rule. It works by estimating how far the model-estimated values are away from the target values and then updates the parameter such that this difference reduces. After several iterations, the difference gets smaller, and once it is small enough, we say our model has learnt the parameters. A figurative explanation is given here:

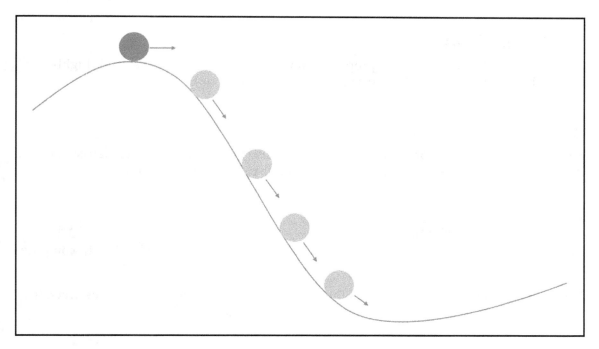

The learning of the model is similar to a rolling ball. It is an iterative process, and after each process, the parameters are updated. The update pushes the parameters to minimize an `objective` function. This minimization is represented as pushing the ball downwards on the slope. The best parameters are equivalent to model state at the bottom of the slope.

Useful tools

In this section, we will see some of the tools that are used while creating machine learning models. Here, we will be using the scikit-learn package, but these are available in many other libraries too. The overall functioning and the purpose remain the same.

Preprocessing

Preprocessing the input as well as target labels in settings such as classification or regression is as important as the model itself. Some of the techniques used are explained as follows.

Normalization

For the ease of the model to learn proper parameters through a training set, it is highly essential to normalize the values in a small range, usually 0 to 1.

Noise

For making the system more robust, the input can also be added with small Gaussian noise. In the case of images as input, the noise corresponds to salt and pepper noise.

Postprocessing

In the case of classification, the output of the model is an array of probabilities. To compute the predicted label for the input, we use an index with the maximum value of the array.

In the case of regression, the output of the model is usually normalized values between the range 0-1. This requires rescaling of the output to the original domain.

Evaluation

Once we have trained a model, to evaluate, it is highly necessary to check its overall validity. In a binary classification problem, setting the evaluation is done by using the following output values. Here, we want to evaluate the model's performance for category A:

- **True positive (TP)**: Given a sample from label A, the output is also categorized as A
- **True negative (TN)**: Given a sample from label A, the output is categorized into B
- **False positive (FP)**: Given a sample from label B, the output is categorized into A
- **False negative (FN)**: Given a sample from B, the output is also categorized into B

This is done for the evaluation set, and based on it, we compute the following parameters.

Precision

The precision value tells us how much the result is relevant to our goal in accuracy. This is computed as follows:

$$\text{Precision} = \frac{\text{TP}}{\text{TP} + \text{TN}}$$

Using scikit-learn, we can do this as:

```
from sklearn.metrics import precision_score
true_y = .... # ground truth values
pred_y = .... # output of the model


precision = precision_score(true_y, pred_y, average='micro')
```

Recall

Recall tells us how many of the results are truly relevant. This is computed as follows:

$$\text{Recall} = \frac{\text{TP}}{\text{TP} + \text{FN}}$$

Using scikit-learn:

```
from sklearn.metrics import recall_score
true_y = .... # ground truth values
pred_y = .... # output of the model


recall = recall_score(true_y, pred_y, average='micro')
```

F-measure

Using both the precision and recall values, F-measure (specifically F1-score for the overall evaluation) is computed. This is given as follows:

$$\text{F1-score} = 2.\frac{\text{Precision. Recall}}{\text{Precision} + \text{Recall}}$$

Using scikit-learn, this can be computed as:

```
from sklearn.metrics import f1_score
true_y = .... # ground truth values
pred_y = .... # output of the model


f1_value = f1_score(true_y, pred_y, average='micro')
```

Summary

In this chapter, an overview of machine learning was explained with relevant tools. The explanation here complements several algorithms presented in the chapter.

Taking into account the curse of dimensionality, learning overview, and evaluation of the model, we can create better computer vision applications that use machine learning techniques.

Other Books You May Enjoy

If you enjoyed this book, you may be interested in these other books by Packt:

Machine Learning for OpenCV
Michael Beyeler

ISBN: 978-1-78398-028-4

- Explore and make effective use of OpenCV's Machine Learning module
- Learn deep learning for computer vision with Python
- Master linear regression and regularization techniques
- Classify objects such as flower species, handwritten digits, and pedestrians
- Explore the effective use of support vector machines, boosted decision trees, and random forests
- Get acquainted with neural networks and Deep Learning to address real-world problems
- Discover hidden structures in your data using k-means clustering
  Get to grips with data pre-processing and feature engineering

Computer Vision with Python 3
Saurabh Kapur

ISBN: 978-1-78829-976-3

- Working with open source libraries such Pillow, Scikit-image, and OpenCV
- Writing programs such as edge detection, color processing, image feature extraction, and more
- Implementing feature detection algorithms like LBP and ORB
- Tracking objects using an external camera or a video file
- Optical Character Recognition using Machine Learning.
- Understanding Convolutional Neural Networks to learn patterns in images
- Leveraging Cloud Infrastructure to provide Computer Vision as a Service

Leave a review - let other readers know what you think

Please share your thoughts on this book with others by leaving a review on the site that you bought it from. If you purchased the book from Amazon, please leave us an honest review on this book's Amazon page. This is vital so that other potential readers can see and use your unbiased opinion to make purchasing decisions, we can understand what our customers think about our products, and our authors can see your feedback on the title that they have worked with Packt to create. It will only take a few minutes of your time, but is valuable to other potential customers, our authors, and Packt. Thank you!

Index